CW00545837

THE WORLD IS EVER CHANGING

in association with

STUDIOCANAL

BRITISH ACADEMY
OF FILM AND TELEVISION ARTS

The World Is Ever Changing

NICOLAS ROEG

faber and faber

First published in this edition in 2013
by Faber and Faber Limited
Bloomsbury House,
74–77 Great Russell Street,
London WC1B 3DA

Typeset by Faber and Faber Ltd

Printed and bound by CPI Group (UK) Ltd, Croydon, CR0 4YY

The right of Nicolas Roeg to be identified as author
of this work has been asserted in accordance with Section 77
of the Copyright, Designs and Patents Act 1988

*This book is sold subject to the condition that it shall not,
by way of trade or otherwise, be lent, resold, hired out
or otherwise circulated without the publisher's prior consent
in any form of binding or cover other than that in which
it is published and without a similar condition including
this condition being imposed on the subsequent purchaser*

A CIP record for this book
is available from the British Library

ISBN 978-0-571-26493-3

FSC
www.fsc.org
MIX
Paper from
responsible sources
FSC® C101712

2 4 6 8 10 9 7 5 3 1

Contents

Prologue   1

Beginnings   7

Image   27

Sound   39

Script   55

Directing   79

Actors   103

Producers   127

Editing   141

Love Scenes   157

Mirrors   173

The Future   191

Disjecta Membra   203

Filmography   239

Credits   244

Prologue

Graffiti found where I shot *Performance*

What follows is not a lecture. It is how I feel about some of
the aspects of the great love of my life, who was born only a
few years before me, and how we grew up together from my
early adolescence, growing from a young love at first sight to
a great, deep, abiding and admired enchantment for me: the
cinema. Movies.

The motion picture is still such a magical and mysterious
combination of reality, art, science and the supernatural – as
well as a gateway to the nature of Time, and perhaps even
the first clue in solving the puzzle of what we're doing here
on this world.

Its importance is very underrated.

Coupled to this is the fact that the speed of development
is accelerating at a rate, in terms of mental and physical abil-
ities, our life expectancy can hardly cope with.

Economically, we are trapped manufacturing things that
are already out of date; which hints at the thought that prac-
ticality, reality and physicality lead us astray and away from
truths we aren't ready for. My belief is that we are a lot
closer to some giant changes in understanding the 'Blake-
like' meaning of life and the time conundrum than we can
recognise. The capturing of the shadows of everything and

everyone makes time a moveable feast with no beginning, middle and end, as we now know it.

My thoughts are the 'bio' of my life. They are in no form of time or continuity. There is no better lure to help us than the entrapment of the moving image that we can see again and again and even repeat in a different way that can please us more when seen as another aspect of the truth. 'The Truth? What is that?' said jesting Pilate . . . and didn't wait for an answer.

Pilate would have understood the story the actor Richard Johnson once told me. He and Sir Laurence Olivier were having a drink together between a matinee and an evening performance in Stratford-on-Avon of a Shakespeare play in which they were both performing. They were moaning to each other about a similar crisis they were both experiencing in their private lives when Olivier suddenly said – 'Oh, enough of this, Richard, it's getting late. We should really forget this now and get back to the theatre and the "Real World". I know exactly what he means and I hope you and I will meet again in a couple of pages' time.

If and before we do, I would like to add one more thought for you to take with you. This is not an excuse, but more of a confession. Obviously more than half the chapters are about my feelings and memories of the past and my understanding of the memory of things. Memory has no continuity of time so don't worry about reading it in any progressive order.

I hope the unfolding of my life, hopes and dreams in this way doesn't have too much of a sense of order (or too little). Perhaps the last chapter 'The Future' will help the scattered

fragments of connected thoughts. Together with the photographs of the notes I've made over the years that are in no particular order on the desk, it may say something of the magic of the captured moving image, that is for me the most magical ability I can think of. It has already, and still does, open doors of revelation which will finally show us the future. The future that in the 'time conundrum' has already happened.

The movies have embraced every art form and every way of telling a story, both in fiction and reality – whatever that is. We are now about to enter another era of existence.

Who knows? Maybe future space travellers will simply find the earth inhabited by shadows from what we call our past.

Beginnings

Where was I born? I was born at home. It was in 1928 – 15 August, quite a good day, Napoleon's birthday, but I like to think Napoleon was born on my birthday. And at quite an apposite name for a place – Circus Road. 31 Circus Road, St John's Wood, London.

Then everything suddenly went downhill for the family and we moved to Brighton and Hove when I was . . . I must have been about three or four maybe. I went to school there in Hove and then moved up to London at a curious time – 1940, just before the Blitz started! All through the war I went to school in London, until I was seventeen, when I volunteered to go into the forces.

All through my boyhood I'd wanted to go into the Air Force. I wanted to fly. But then the war ended and they weren't taking any more trainee pilots. They had enough, so I went into the army and joined the Airborne, served my time with the 16th Independent Parachute Brigade.

When I left the army, it was too late to go to university. At first I got a job in Marylebone Studios. They were opposite the flat I was living in and I kind of knew the son of the owner. It was fascinating. I knew nothing about movies. I knew I liked them, but I had no idea about them

Dressed as a hussar for a wedding

at all. I was completely innocent. Today, it's very difficult for anybody to be completely innocent about the idea

of the retained image. But, then, there weren't any film schools and, of course, there weren't any sort of 'media studies' courses at all as far as film was concerned. It was more like apprenticeships. They drew directors mainly from the theatre. And, certainly in England, theatre was the dramatic medium at the time, not cinema – film was thought rather less of. There was a snobbish attitude in England. The actors were, 'Yes, I'm doing a film, but I'm expecting to do a play in a month's time – I just thought it would be amusing to do a film.' There was a sense that film actors were looked down on. Gradually, England, as well as France, became more film-conscious, though not as much as in America. Curiously enough, Britain has still kept the great tradition of the theatre.

Technically, things are changing so swiftly now that thanks to the computer, young people can make films much more easily; their dealings in the exchange of images with each other is much greater than it ever was before. But when I was young I had no idea how film was put together nor what it did. The very first film I remember – or the very first shot – was in a Laurel and Hardy film. I think it was *Babes in Toyland*. They were both lying in bed – in the same bed, a double bed. No comment was ever made about that . . . two men in nightshirts lying next to each other in bed – it was great, it was totally accepted then, before 'political correctness' happened. Anyway, a feather came down on Ollie's nose, and he blew it. It was a rather marvellous little effect shot, this feather going up and coming down and landing on the other's nose. Then it went to one of them – I think it was Stan – who swallowed it and started laughing.

I really liked going to the cinema. I went with my sister. She liked going to the movies, or going to 'the pictures' – in England, it wasn't called 'the movies' then. There was a continuous performance, and she used to make me sit through it: 'Let's sit through the next showing till it comes round again.' And we'd sit through it and she'd say, 'Oh, I loved that scene.' That must have been about the time I first became seduced by the cinema. My fate was sealed.

My first job was at Marylebone Studios where I made the tea and did general errands – and watched films. They did a lot of films for the Ministry of Information, but they were never shown in the cinemas. Then I moved on to a cutting room run by a friend of the owner of Marylebone Studios, a man called Major De Lane Lea. He'd been in British intelligence in France and he ran a French dubbing studio in Wardour Street called Lingua Synchrome, which became De Lane Lea, which then became quite a famous place for post-production. He's dead now – tragically committed suicide, for unknown reasons. They worked on films that were already made – mainly dubbing French films into English. I saw a lot of French films, obviously, and was very impressed by a film directed by Marcel Carné – *Les Enfants du Paradis*. I think it was made in 1945, just at the end of the war. I'd never seen anything like it.

People always ask what film has influenced me – well, everything in life influences you. Somehow we're all feasting off each other in some way and twisting it to our own devices and intentions, but *Les Enfants du Paradis* was full of things that constantly enchanted me. The film has many stories – all the characters have different stories and they're all joined together. All things are connected in life, but we all have our different stories – our friends, our relations, our husbands and wives – and connected with this is the sense of time passing. It's a form I've always been drawn to – the individual and their part in society. You have your own personal story, as well as being connected to someone else's.

And how close does one get to someone else? It comes down to the question I've asked many times: 'What are you thinking, darling?' The answer given is nearly always different from what they are *really* thinking. I think the performances in *Puffball* are extraordinary for that reason. There are four women, at four different ages – and with four very different attitudes towards sex. The characters all have different reasons for their behaviour, attitudes, hopes and dreams, different reasons for what they want to do. They seem to be part of a family, but the joy of Miranda Richardson's character at the end of the film is completely unconnected to the other characters' endings in the story. She's happy, whereas the husband of Kelly Reilly is not. But each of them have been truthful to their inner souls.

When we were shooting it, people would say to me, 'I don't know where we are in the story, Nic. That doesn't connect with what's happening to the other characters.' But it does connect – they're all the same character, but in a different position. It's a joint story – a joint story within a shell inhabited by all these different people. They all come to this one location for different reasons. Similarly with *Les Enfants du Paradis* – three very different individuals who are connected to each other and the society around them.

The odd thing about that – I only realised it much later – is that Marcel Carné entered the film business in 1928, the year I was born. He was born in 1909, on 18 August, and curiously enough, he began as a camera assistant as well. I mean, coincidence is coincidence, but I find these coincidences of film-making rather marvellous.

Initially, when I went to De Lane Lea, I was just getting the tea and writing down the translations. De Lane Lea had a special system for dubbing, using a machine called an Editola. It looked rather like a big television set. There were two reels of film going through the machine. One went over

The Editola (Courtesy of North West Film Archive
at Manchester Metropolitan University)

14

the picture head and the other went over the sound head. And there was a handle in the middle so that as you turned it, the film could go forwards or backwards – you could shift the speed around, you could slow it down or speed it up. Just seeing a character going forwards and backwards, up and down, expanded my thoughts about what you could do with images. I couldn't wait to get on the Editola.

I was in a very lowly position, just marking up places on the tape where labials came up – the m's and b's and p's – so that they could then try to fit 'my' with '*moi*' and 'bag' with '*package*'. But during lunch hour and after work I'd stay on and ask the chief editor to lace up something on the Editola so I could have a look at it, and she'd always say yes. She was a very nice woman – Gladys Bremson. Running it backwards and forwards fascinated me – life passing and then returning, passing and returning; someone gets shot and then gets back up again. I realised that there was another way of telling stories, of passing on information – not on the page, but through the retention of the image, the moving image. This is such an extraordinary thing. We're used to it now, but it still excites me because this whole idea of connecting film with our minds is still unexplored. In the novel you can write 'he thought', as in '"My God, what a beautiful pair of legs she has," he thought.' In a film it's called a flashback – but it comes from the book form. The only difference being in a movie it is 'said' with an image and in a book it is 'said' with a word. But in film we can play with images and the retention of the image in an extraordinary way. In life we have a clash of realities that is quite magnificent: as I'm dictating to the camera now, I'm also looking out of the window and thinking, and then remembering when that tree outside was a little tree, when it was planted, which in turn prompts other thoughts. One can do that with film (I must stop calling it 'film'. My grandchildren won't even know what the word means and it will take too long to explain it.) in a way that you can't really do with anything else. You can't put it as effectively on the page; you can't capture it in any other way. Film has nothing to do with the theatre because the theatre is driven by language – but film is not driven by language, it's driven by image.

I remember my father coming back from the cinema after seeing *Citizen Kane*, saying, 'What was all that business about the sledge?' It was another form of telling a story, one that is different from the literary form. A boy looks at a sledge, he sees 'Rosebud' – what the hell is 'Rosebud'? It was completely baffling to people, but nowadays it's so clear that you probably wouldn't even have that shot. I'm happy that movies have such a long life because people can be confounded at first by what they see, especially if it goes against the conventions of the time – and the studio.

So I'd get on the Editola and run the tape back and forth, changing things, making movies for myself, like with this game *Heavy Rain*, where you can remake the movie for yourself. So the Editola was like a PlayStation 3 for me. And, most crucially, I was beginning to think of film as another form of storytelling. In *Walkabout* there's a scene where the boy sees two Australian hunters come by and he doesn't want to be seen by them, so he hides behind a bush. He watches as they take their rifles and shoot a wild creature. The boy sees it collapse. And when we were editing that scene, I remember thinking back to the time I was playing around with the Editola, when I was able to make the action go forwards and backwards. I also remembered that there was a scene in Cocteau's *Beauty and the Beast* where the image suddenly spools backwards and the beast suddenly comes back to life. So in *Walkabout* I had the animal that had just been shot come back to life again. But when I made the film, this sort of thing was considered 'tricksy'. People didn't think you could, or should, use film in that way – as a way of reflecting what was in a character's mind. The boy didn't want the animal to die, so in his head he made him come alive again – and I could show what was going on in his mind by having it stand up again.

At the time people thought I was crazy, but as time has passed people have recognised it as a way of showing what's going on in the imagination. There's not a right way of doing something and a wrong way. There's a right way – and another way. So let's take a chance on the other way.

So, I was working at De Lane Lea, going up and down Wardour Street, getting sandwiches for the editor, having discussions in the pub with this new kind of society – people who were involved with films who became friends, mates. Then I went to France with De Lane Lea because he wanted to shoot a documentary. It was in the south, by the Pyrenees, near the border with Spain. It was semi-holiday, semi-work. He wanted to get some shots of border guards. What was fascinating was that I'd never seen a movie camera before. Of course I'd seen them, but never this close, working on location. I basically just carried the camera around. When we got back, he was going through all sorts of troubles, which led to his suicide. Gladys Bremson's husband had just started the ACT – the film technician's union – and they had a little two-page journal which came out monthly. It told you what was happening in the industry, and there was an advertisement for a job at the MGM studios in Borehamwood for clapper loaders. So I went over to the studio and was interviewed by Freddie Young, the brilliant head cameraman under contract to MGM, and he said, 'Can you start on Monday?' So on Monday morning I found myself in the loading room right next to the sound stage learning how to load a film magazine in the dark. I didn't think I wanted to be a cameraman. It was more a case of, 'So that's how they make films.' I just drifted into it. I never really transferred from one department to another; I just knew I wanted to make films. I had a line in *Eureka*: 'You fell into life, Claude,' the girl says in the film. I think that is so true ... I think I fell into life too.

In those days, getting a job at a studio was like getting a job in a factory – they'd advertise the jobs. If people went into movies to get work on the camera, they'd go up to the studio and see the chief cameraman or the chief loader and get a job in the loading room. So a whole new chapter in learning the trade began. It's from the trade that the art grew. Take the Raphael paintings, which were often done by his apprentices, some of whom went on to become great artists themselves, while others remained great tradesmen – you know, 'He's wonderful with cloaks.' I really valued my apprentice-

As a focus puller (first assistant cameraman) to the right of the camera, shooting Joan Collins and James Kenney in *Cosh Boy* with Lewis Gilbert to my left

ship: in order to change things, to go against the conventions imposed by the studio, you have to know how to do it in the first place, you have to know what the conventions of the time are.

The studio where I got the job was the London branch of the big MGM outfit in Los Angeles, so it was a major film studio – another existence altogether different from anything I had experienced before. It was the first time I saw huge sets being built, a whole different world being created for the camera. It was magical. Studio work is very exciting because it's a matched reality – it isn't as straightforward as going out to shoot in the actual place.

It was also the first time I saw actors at work. I worked on

Greer Garson in *The Miniver Story*

The Miniver Story – a sequel to *Mrs Miniver* – and watched Greer Garson and Walter Pidgeon. I thought, 'There's something strange going on here.' They were completely different from the British actors. Gradually, I did other movies and realised the difference was because the American actors were working from a tradition of film. They hadn't been to drama school. I think Clark Gable had worked on oil wells. I did a little bit with Gable on a Delmer Daves film called *Never Let Me Go*, and he was very nervous, especially if he had to say lines – He would say, 'I'm not going to talk.' I noticed American actors would always give lines away to the British actors. In a scene a girl would come into the room, and in the script the character played by the American star would say, 'Oh hello, how are you? Glad to meet you.' And if there was an English actor – let's say Charles Kingsland or someone like that – then the American actor would say, 'Don't you think it would be better if Charles said "Hello" to her, and "Come in," and then "Sit down," and I just watch her and she looks at me and I look back at her? I think Charles would say the line so much better than me.' Of course, the English actor would be flattered: 'You think so? OK, I'll say it: Oh, do come in and sit down.' Of course, Charles didn't realise that when it comes to the cutting room, his line – 'Come in and sit down' – will be off-screen, and on-screen Clark Gable will be looking at the girl as she comes in, and she'll be looking at him, while Charles's voice is being heard off-screen. It'll be about the reactions. That's completely different from the theatre, where you can't help looking at the person who's speaking. Great screen acting is more often reacting than performing.

What they call 'Pinteresque' pauses are really from film-making. They used to play excerpts from films on the radio, and there'd be long gaps between the words: a character would say 'Hello', then get up and go to the other room to make some tea – gap, gap – while the other person occupies himself by looking through books on a shelf – gap, gap. In the film, they'd cut to the title of the book as the other character is making the tea. 'Do you want anything?' says the character making the tea. The other character continues looking through the book: 'What? No.' So there are big gaps that couldn't exist on the stage because you wouldn't be able to cut away to what the man's reading.

The theatre has a completely different structure from cinema – even today. The tradition of the theatre, which is a splendid tradition, has nothing to do with movies. Just by watching and serving my apprenticeship I realised how huge this difference was. In film the audience is picked up and taken outside to look at something in the street, as I see it through my window, and then they're brought back in – the images drive the plot, the images drive the action. Words cover up a lot of embarrassment, truths, inner thoughts, all kinds of things – but the cinema works in a completely different way. Our stories move forward much more on a lateral than a linear fashion. Time goes by, while the story is broadening or shrinking.

An extraordinary thing happened to me at that time – it was in a restaurant called 'La Caprice' – I was there with my sister and brother-in-law and I went down to the gents at some point during the dinner – I was an assistant or maybe a camera operator by then; it was the early fifties. I had a quick pee and then was washing my hands – and standing next to me was Jacob Epstein! I couldn't believe it, I loved his work – the strength and power of it, the fury of life in it. He was well thought of, but I don't think he's ever been really recognised as the genius he was.

I was in a state of shock. I didn't know what to do; I looked at him and he was sort of mumbling to himself, and I said, 'I just love your work.' And he said, 'Oh, good' – or something like that. I found a piece of paper and said, 'Would you sign this for me?' and he said, 'What! Have I no privacy anywhere!' He went into a tirade – the toilet was downstairs and I went back upstairs – and I hadn't realised he was dining at a table a little further along. Epstein was cutting between the tables, saying, 'Why do I have to have this young man asking me in the lavatory to sign something? Can I have no peace or privacy?'

My sister, Nicolette, said, 'What on earth did you do down there?' I said, 'I asked him for his signature.' She said, 'Oh, Christ!' He was sitting with two young women – I think one of them was his daughter – and he pointed at me: 'He's the one.' And the waiter came over and said, 'I think you ought to go now,' and I said, 'I haven't had my dinner.' Then the waiter came back and said, 'I think he's too crazed to calm down,' and we went home.

A couple of days later I was telling the story to a friend of mine called Kevin Kavanagh and we were laughing about it and I said perhaps there is a right way and a wrong way of behaving – manners maketh the man. I knew, in some way, that I'd been stupid. I think Epstein had just been knighted, so I wrote a little fable about a squire at a jousting tournament – he's the squire to a knight and he asks the knight for one of the favours worn by one of the ladies sitting in the royal box , and the knight says, 'I can't do that for you now, but after the match I could. Come and talk to me about it then, because it would be very bad of me to ask for it now.' It was just a little story illustrating that there's a right way and a wrong way of doing everything, in terms of behaviour and manners. You can't be blunt or rude – you affect people's hopes and dreams. We wrote out the story . . . put it in an envelope . . . found out where Epstein lived and Kevin and I drove down there and popped it through his door. I signed it: From the Page Boy in the Tent Flap of the Caprice. We just laughed about it and went and had a drink. I still adored his work – his *Jacob and the Angel* is just fantastic.

The strangest thing of all was that a couple of years later he died, and I was in Marylebone, taking some clothes to the cleaners, and there was a big buzz outside the shop – police cars and motorcycles went by – and I went to the door of the cleaners and said, 'What's happening?' and they said, 'Oh, it's Epstein's funeral' and, just at that moment, his coffin went by me in the hearse – I was stunned – and as it passed I waved goodbye to him. I thought, 'How strange that I should be right here at this moment.'

Then, some years later, I was telling the story as a sort of joke at a cocktail party and I was talking to this man, who turned out to be a psychiatrist and he said, 'Well, I'll be damned, that story tells me a lot of things.' I said, 'What do you mean?' It turned out that Epstein was a patient or a friend of his and he said, 'He had a complete change of attitude a few years ago, he was less gruff. I can see now that you must have prompted that change.'

I thought: 'That's an extraordinary thing' – my fandom had turned into something quite useful. I had helped Jacob Epstein to be a nicer man!

I think all fan letters to anyone who has a public image – however well known or important – are really quite affecting. They usually come from complete strangers or people one has bumped into by chance at a reception or even stood next to in an elevator. I have had them – good and bad – of course, not in the numbers that actors or more publicly known figures get. However, they nearly always prompt a feeling in me of being obliged to answer them – although I'm not sure that those who send them really expect a reply.

Obviously, there is something of the critic about them and one should never respond to critics. But my brush with the great Jacob Epstein only serves to show that I've been a fan myself and perhaps it's not always wise to respond to strangers – but I still think he was brilliant.

I was a camera operator on a movie called *Tarzan's Greatest Adventure*. The producer was quite an amusing guy, and I said to him, 'The title's a superlative! You won't be able to make any more afterwards!' *Tarzan's Disappointing Adventure* would have to be the next one. But it was a lot of fun. Tarzan was played by Gordon Scott. He was a terrifically nice man and really very, very bright – an awfully nice guy. One thing was quite funny: we were shooting in Kenya, and Tarzan had to run through the jungle. As he couldn't wear plimsoles or little shoes, they made 'feet' for him – they were like tight stockings made of rubber. They looked like his feet from the bottom just up to his ankles, and they blended in and had artificial hair on them so he could run in the jungle, jumping on trees and swinging and landing on the ground – they were padded underneath. We were shooting out in the bush somewhere outside Nairobi. Some of the local people had never seen films – certainly not films being made with actors – and they were fascinated. Of course, they could run through the jungle without shoes just like anyone who was used to it – I know I could run without shoes over the stones on the beach when I was a young boy in Brighton – so the locals, watching the filming, not realising or knowing anything about shoes that looked like bare feet, had accepted that someone was running in the jungle without shoes. Anyway, we did a couple of shots, and they were watching and laughing and trying to chat to Gordon, and he said, 'Oh God, I've got to have a break.' He sat down in his chair, lifted his leg and started taking his feet off! And they looked at him as he tore these feet off – and they ran away! 'Aaah!' They thought he'd been terribly hurt – it was fantastic and understandable. That's the magic of the movies. Now, of course, he wouldn't be running in reality at all; he'd be doing it on the stage against a blue screen, and they'd put it on with CGI and goodness knows what. He wouldn't have to have artificial feet with the wardrobe department boasting, 'We've got a good idea: we can make these rubber shoes that'll look like feet.' (Actually, thinking about it, it probably is still a good idea – maybe.)

Time went by. Movies were marching on and commercials were coming in and television and goodness knows what, but right at the beginning of that I'd started to light film as director of photography – though it was called 'cameraman' then.

Image

As director of photography on *Far From the Madding Crowd*

Thank goodness I started as a cameraman on black-and-white movies like *Dr Crippen*, with Samantha Eggar and Donald Pleasence. Black and white has an extraordinarily different aesthetic from colour. Colour has its own balance, but to bring beauty to it or drama or threat is more difficult, in many ways, than with black and white; on the other hand, black and white is more difficult to approach in terms of the actual photography than colour. The balance of things in

As director of photography on *The Caretaker*
with Robert Shaw and Donald Pleasance

black and white is more difficult. Colour, on the other hand, seems very simple to do, because the basic shot, once you've got the exposure correct, always seems to balance itself. But though colour is in many ways simpler to capture, it's more difficult to create a sense of atmosphere with it.

Black and white was accepted by people because it was artificial. Unless you're colour-blind, people generally see the world in colour, so you can do extraordinary things with black and white: you can have shafts of very bright light or dark lines on a person's face, all of which would look very artificial in colour. Curiously enough, black and white became 'artistic' instead of 'artificial'. Black and white somehow entered the consciousness; you could get away with much more extravagant invention in terms of the image than you could with colour. And because I'd had this training, photographing in black and white, I was uninhibited by suddenly having to work in colour; on the contrary, it was exciting to me. I thought, 'How can we make colour more dramatic, what shall we do?' We didn't have computerisation then; it had to be done inside the camera or with the lighting. So it gave me a chance to try and make the image as interesting and acceptable in colour as it was in black and white.

I remember one film I was shooting – I was on the camera, pulling focus. We were on location – Piccadilly, Regent Street, somewhere around there – and we'd had to get police permission to shut off the streets and get barriers set up. A little boy was standing there watching us shoot, and his mother said to me – we were having a break, the crew were having a cup of tea and I was standing by the camera – she said, 'Can he have a look?' and I said, 'Of course,' and lifted the boy up, and he looked through the camera and moved the handles to pan it round. As I put him down, his mother asked, 'Can I have a look too?' 'Be quick,' I said. And she got up on the camera, and as she looked through she said, 'Oh, it's in colour, is it?' She was looking through the camera expecting the image to be in black and white! She hadn't associated the camera with seeing the world as she saw it with her own eyes. Black and white was what was most natural in films.

Of course, the first problem was: how would you capture colour on celluloid? And once that was solved, colour tended to be used for grander films – like *Gone with the Wind*. People went to see the movie for the colour. You can't imagine *The Wizard of Oz* without the colour – the yellow of the brick road, the red of Dorothy's shoes. Ordinary life, on the other hand, was black and white. It seems strange now, but people didn't really translate the life they saw around them – which was in colour – into what they expected to see on the screen.

You have to be very careful when you use colour. Particular colours are very closely associated with the nature of things. It was very interesting shooting *A Funny Thing Happened on the Way to the Forum* for Richard Lester. It had originally been a play, and the sets for the film were more like theatre sets. Obviously, sets are specially built for films, but in this case they were going to be used in a 'theatrical' way. The main actors, like Zero Mostel and Phil Silvers, were theatre actors. The scenes were very theatrical – the source material was the plays of the Roman dramatist, Plautus. And

As director of photography on *A Funny Thing
Happened on the Way to the Forum*

I said to Richard Lester, 'Why don't we shoot it for its the-atricality – making it brighter on the people, but virtually burnt out in the background?' Richard said, 'Let's try it.' So we shot it that way, and again I ran into trouble with the producers. They said, 'We've seen the rushes and it's all burnt out in the background.' And I said, 'Yes, it's beautiful. It gives a kind of 3D look to it.' It had a reality to it. For one of the dinner scenes it was very bright on the characters, so you weren't caught up in 'What an extraordinary set!' They weren't playing up to the setting, they were acting and react-ing to each other.

The lab sent notes back to me: 'The close-ups are great, but we're just warning you that the shots are burnt out at the back.' When you look at the film today, you wouldn't think there was anything wrong with it. You should make films for the future – if you do that, the audience will catch up with you, eventually.

I shot *The Masque of the Red Death* for Roger Corman. There's an extraordinary brilliance to Roger, but he didn't want to be thought of in any way as an artist. In his mind, they were just B-pictures. We shot it at a hell of a pace – three and a half weeks. At the end, he said to me, 'Is there another movie you want to do, Nic? Because instead of tearing down these sets, we could use them again.' Red was the central theme of the film, so we gradually built up the use of red – the sacrificial sense of red – until it dominated. Patently, red's an incredibly strong colour. Originally, pink was the colour for a boy and blue for a girl: blue was innocence; pink was the forerunner of red, the forerunner of the violence and strength of the adult male. In our use of red, we were guided by the dictum that the photography tells the story and doesn't call attention to itself.

I had been an assistant to a marvellous old American cameraman, Joe Ruttenberg. He was a Hollywood cameraman who came to England to photograph *The Miniver Story* because Greer Garson wanted him; he'd photographed her before, and she thought he was wonderful. He was an extraordinary man, and I learned a lot from him. He said, 'You must never forget, Nic, you're not out to win any award from the Royal Photographic Society with the movie. It's the story you're trying to inject with feeling, with an attitude, not the photography. If the audience has been

frightened by the look of it, they won't know it, they won't say, "Oh, that shot frightened me because it looked so strange." The fear would be inside them and the photography won't be noticed.'

Once the look became part of the story, the story became part of the look; the look was driving the story, it was separating itself from the written word. An image can make more emotional sense than words because it helps the imagination on its way visually rather than just by interpretation. This whole idea of connecting film with our minds is still relatively unexplored. We're still connecting it in some archaic way with the structure of the novel.

I made a film called *The Witches*. Interestingly, Roald Dahl's book was rather creepy but it had very simple, sweet, charming drawings in it – so that the children wouldn't get too frightened. If a parent were reading the story to a child and saw the child getting nervous about it or upset, they could shut the book, but once you take someone into the cinema and put them in a seat, you frighten the bejesus out of them. And I had been rather wild in terms of the images, much wilder than the Quentin Blake images in the book, and I had made the end quite scary. It was one of the few occasions I didn't mind the studio actually wanting to change the ending. Curiously enough, when Dahl saw it the first time he didn't mind it at all.

Children are much more sophisticated than one thinks. They're aware of much more, they can accept extraordinary images. I remember running some rushes from *The Witches* at home on VHS, and one of my young sons started watching it and then ran round and sat behind the television set. In fact, I took out a lot of stuff that was quite extraordinary, but I'm only saying this to illustrate how the image can be much more frightening than the word. Much more frightening. Much more thought provoking. It's different from the word.

Size is different as well. When I was making *Eureka*, we had the rushes sent out to us in the West Indies and then in northern Canada, and then way up in the north in Alaska, in the snow. I was running the rushes on VHS – sitting in front of a screen, but a screen whose size you dominate, physically dominate, so somehow, subconsciously, the action reduces itself as well. A man wandering in the desert is less awesome when you're in front of a TV screen rather than sitting in a cinema, where there's a huge screen and a tiny figure and you're a tiny figure as well watching the action. Size makes it a completely different emotional experience. I noticed that when I was watching one of the scenes, I kept thinking, 'When we set up the next day, maybe if we get closer . . .' But 'No' – I got a grip on myself. I reminded myself, 'This is for the cinema.' Some films, some shots are only really going to have their effect in a cinema.

Young people now can spot, instantly, which is a movie and which is a film made for television. There's something that happens through the editing, of course, but visually there are certain things that just don't work as well emotionally on a small screen as they do on a big screen. I learned that sort of thing through progressing through the expansion of the whole idea of the retained image, whether it's on television, on your mobile phone or on the cinema screen; they're all different delivery systems that have different needs and criteria.

Sound

The first commercial film with sound was *The Jazz Singer*, with Al Jolson. He said at the beginning, 'You ain't heard nothing yet,' and then sang the song, 'Mammy' – that was in 1927. And I find it extraordinary that in that same year Abel Gance had just finished a gigantic, extraordinary mega-movie – *Napoleon*, a picture of tremendous innovation where the image had done all kinds of things: he had a camera on a horse's back, he had a camera on a bungee wire – such extraordinary movement – he had shots on three screens running at the same time, and, of course, an orchestra in the theatre providing the sound of hail falling on the soldiers' drums – but no sound from the screen, no spoken dialogue, just title cards interspersed with the visual sequences. But the images were astounding, even today. And playing the role of Marat was Antonin Artaud, the French poet, playwright, actor and surrealist whose Theatre of Cruelty expressed things by gesture. He despised the word; he thought the word was less powerful than the gesture and the look and the behaviour. Abel Gance planned to do two or three films of Napoleon's life, but this was really the last great silent movie.

Napoleon: shots on three screens at the same time

Then sound came in. After *The Jazz Singer*, there was a whole revolution in the use of picture and sound, and it put the image back because the sound had to be catered for. They had to put the camera in big soundproof cabins because of the noise it made: 'Everyone on the set be quiet!' – the camera was turning. They didn't have what became known as a 'blimp' around the camera – that was the next stage, which allowed the camera to move again. But Gance had just finished this gigantic film with images telling the story in an astounding way, and the coming of sound held up the development of people reading the film, reading the picture for . . . well, almost until today.

When sound came in, film began to lose its meaning as the images began to be abandoned in the storytelling process. The studios turned to authors. At the time there wasn't such a thing as a screenwriter, really – they worked from scenarios, where things were just sketched out. So they turned to the East Coast, to novelists, playwrights and journalists, and films became obsessed with the word – for years and years and years – until suddenly a change came about with a new generation of film-makers who were reading the images, reading the story through pictures.

I remember when I was an assistant on *Bhowani Junction* – the George Cukor film with Stewart Granger and Ava Gardner. We were in India/Pakistan – it was just after Partition – and we were shooting in this railway station in Lahore and crowds were there. People were trying to control them, and I was watching and talking to the Indian grip. A man arrived on the corner of the platform and started unwrapping a candle. He was talking all the time, and I said, 'What's he doing?' The grip told me, 'He's a storyteller,' and the man put out various things: a little book and then a necklace and then a little curved knife. He lit the candle and, as he was talking, people came and sat and watched for a while. They'd throw a couple of rupees onto the floor, and he'd nod to them and go on with his story and doing things with the pieces that he'd taken out of a bag. He sat there the whole morning, talking. I said, 'This is fantastic. What's the story?' 'It's ever changing,' came the reply. The story changed all the time – and so did the pictures. I was fascinated by how he was putting these things down, how the images were being put in front of you – a very ancient form of movie-making.

Although it confused film-makers when it arrived, sound was an extraordinary thing – it's one of the great senses. We wake in the night and hear 'doop, doop, doop, doop-doop' – strange noises. 'It must be a dripping tap, maybe that's it.' So you creep downstairs because you're never really sure – 'Ah, that's OK, someone's left the tap on.'

In *Puffball* there's quite a long sequence – it must be five or six minutes – where I constructed a whole series of shots that built up a scene which was part reality, part the imagination

43

of the characters involved – without a lot of sound effects, but a very accurately reflecting music track where the music – the very roots of the music – was separate from either the story or the actual location of the story. This alien music reflected the internal thoughts of one of the characters. It wasn't a dream – I hate the idea of a 'dream sequence' – it's an event that's also in the imagination of the characters. It starts with the young girl sleeping, and then her bedroom door opens, but because of the state of mind of the girl, I didn't want to make it too overly suspicious – something quite simple – or was it? 'All things are connected' – in ways as yet unknown to us. For all we know, the wind might have caught it or the door wasn't quite on the latch. It just opens. But she links it to the new couple moving in, and she gets up and goes down the stairs and out of the house – and the door closes behind her. Immediately, her mother comes into the corridor – 'Did someone go out, or did I just imagine the sound of the door closing?' It's quite a heavy 'plot' scene but with very little dialogue, and I really wanted it to work that way. We see so much 'narrative' today – everything is explained all the time – and I like to leave something to the imagination.

There's another scene later on when Kelly Reilly is trapped in the cellar – was it an accident, just a fluke, or did someone do it on purpose? There's lots of diverse cuts with the emphasis on different things – a fire burning, a trapdoor locking then unlocking – which add up to a kind of explanation. The sound effects are very spare and almost nothing is said, but you can follow the scene – hopefully – in some way. Television does a lot of explaining, but the more you explain, somehow, the less interested the audience is. The less said the better.

Film is such a powerful medium and it's continually absorbing new thoughts about where to put the emphasis in the sound or the picture, but at each stage of this advance along the continuum of film-making the urge is to make it rigid, and I always feel that it should be more flexible. I'm not against the popular construct, but it's not the only way. When they say that there's a right way and a wrong way, it's tragically inhibiting. I always say that there's a right way and another way – and that way is freedom.

In *Bad Timing* I did a sequence with Theresa Russell and Art Garfunkel where they meet again, or bump into each other, outside the university for the first time since they've been separated in their love affair. They look at each other and they have this short conversation, and I thought, 'What goes on in their heads as they play the scene?' – the shock of meeting again. He looks at her and has a 'thought', and we hear this thought, though his lips don't move. Then he says something that reflects that thought, and then she replies. And when we got the rushes back from the lab there was a note from the man who had processed them: 'It looks a bit out of sync – we've cut some of the sound because their lips weren't moving.' We hadn't alerted him to what we were doing. When the assembler was laying up the soundtracks against the picture, the dialogue didn't match the lip movements – 'Wait a minute, some of the takes must be missing.'

What I was trying to do wasn't common then, and so we reverted to 'the usual' for most of it. The main thing in life is timing – in terms of innovation in thought or the arts. That's how the title of *Bad Timing* came about.

Originally, the film was called *Illusions*; that was the working title. Then we were told that we were going to be sued because it was the same title as a book by Richard Bach, who had written *Jonathan Livingston Seagull*. After we'd settled and withdrawn the title, I was talking to Theresa about one of the scenes, and she said, 'You're crazy! I'm really glad I'm doing this film, I love this movie, but you're pushing them too far, Nic, and I just don't think they're going to eat it.' I love that phrase: 'They're not going to eat it.' And I said, 'What do you mean?' And Theresa said, 'Not me, I think we're doing OK, but you've just got such bad timing.' 'That's a fantastic title,' I said – and that was it: *Bad Timing*. And she was right – I can quote the *Time Out* review: 'There's weird and then there's *Bad Timing*.'

I was doing another movie called *Cold Heaven*. A woman and her husband are on holiday in Mexico and they're out for the day. He goes swimming and a speedboat comes by and he has a terrible accident and is taken to hospital unconscious – and she was about to tell him that she was having an affair and that their marriage is over. We've known about this affair and we've seen her with the lover, who said, 'Are you going to tell him?' 'I might tell him during the holiday.' And she sits in the waiting area of the hospital, and I really want to reveal what's on her mind. So she's just waiting and she doesn't have any expression at all, and you hear the dialogue of her thoughts – just as in *Bad Timing*. You don't see her lips move; you just hear her interior dialogue. And then the doctor comes and says, 'I'm terribly sorry,' and he makes his apologies – there was nothing they could do, etc. And still her thoughts are going, 'What's going to happen now?' And there's one moment, one line I think she says, quite a natural, selfish thing: 'How strange, I'm a widow now.' Not a divorcee, she's a widow – which is rather a good moment.

Gradually – certainly in the last ten or fifteen years – film has been accepted into the fine arts. For instance, as an installation piece. The piece that won Steve McQueen (the director and artist, not the actor) the Turner Prize was based on Buster Keaton's short film about putting a house together and the front of the house falling on top of him. A few years ago I was asked to do a little film by a German producer who was doing something for the BBC, who were doing short films about sound. I didn't quite know what to do, so I said I'd think about it. I started pondering it, and then they said so-and-so was doing one of the films and was playing around with music on a soundtrack, but that seemed all very familiar. And I began to think that we all have our own sound. And, funnily enough, the producer got in touch with some government ministry which was dealing with hidden sounds, sounds that were difficult to trace. They had directional microphones that could go through walls and pick up extraordinary things, like the sound of our bodies.

Our bodies give off sounds, and these sounds can travel great distances, like the way whales communicate with each other. So I became really interested in whale sounds – how they talk to each other from a thousand miles away, how they can make sounds that travel. And I said, 'Let's make something that makes some sort of statement about sound but isn't immediately understood as what people are used to; neither watching nor listening to.' By that, I mean a sound that is not necessarily connected to an image, because that's how life is – you know, we go to a restaurant and we talk to each other across the table and you hear your partner or your friend's voice and that concentrates everything – and subconsciously, of course, you take in the sound of the knife and fork – but then: 'What was that?' You turn round and someone has fainted three tables down, a completely different noise. Well, that's going on to a lesser degree all the time. As our mind concentrates on what we want to hear, we don't hear what maybe we should be hearing or what it's possible for us to hear. And that began to interest me.

The producer who invited me to make a short film for him was also a friend of Claudia Schiffer, a great model. She was the most extraordinary face of the time, an image of the moment, and I thought, 'Why don't we make the "sound" of Claudia Schiffer?' I wrote a sketchy treatment of what we could do with it, prompted by what these people from the government ministry were doing: how inside us we have different sounds – our blood going at different rates at different moments. It's as identifiable as our DNA; it's our own personal soundtrack. On top of which I came to think that this was linked to the origins of film, because movies started with silence, then sound was added. I thought it would be perfect with Claudia Schiffer because nobody had heard her. Here was this extraordinary model that everybody recognised, but she wasn't a performing actress. And this linked her to the silent stars. Mary Pickford was the biggest star of the silent days, one of the founders of United Artists – and nobody had ever heard her speak! I thought, 'There's a link – the sound of Claudia Schiffer is like the sound of Mary Pickford.'

The film ended up about seventeen minutes long. The images focused on her body and we constructed a sound-scape that reflected the sounds of her body. And I wrote a narration which she spoke – Claudia Schiffer speaks! It's like that poster for *Anna Christie*, the first film that Greta Garbo did at the coming of sound – 'Garbo talks!' She survived into the sound era, whereas John Gilbert – her great co-star in the silent era – did not. His high-pitched, squeaky voice was at odds with his dashing, romantic image.

So in the end we did hear Claudia Schiffer. The narration is obviously her, but at the centre of the film are the secret sounds of her body. In fact, it has influenced me right to this day, because we all live secret lives, we all have secret thoughts – and sounds.

I've often said that our thoughts are very different in a lot of ways from what we actually say. And our thoughts about what we hear are very different from what is being said, so there are lots of stories going on in our mind as we try and read people. Usually, sound will fall into a predict-able relationship with the image: this is what is happening and this is what is being said. But we're really just at the tip of the iceberg in terms of sound reaching up to become equal with the image; not abandoning the image, but equal with the image in a different way. Obviously it'll be very difficult to comprehend at first, as anything is that's different. I remember when *Last Year at Marienbad* came out: people just didn't 'get it' at all; then, within three or four years, people finally understood what Alain Resnais was doing. But now things are changing by the month – and our understanding with it. Orson Welles said that speed is the thing that develops the most changes in every form of art, in mankind's progress or development. It's so exciting!

I remember many years ago being in the desert in central Africa, in the southern Sahara, and I remember showing a black-and-white Polaroid photo I had taken of one of the people who were standing and watching us. He took it – looked at it – then turned it upside down. Then one of the others in the group took it, turned it about, and looking back at the first person nodded and laughed, indicating that he recognised it as an image of the first man. Our interpreter, who had been helping to explain the Polaroid, said the men were from a very isolated nomadic tribe and they'd never seen a photograph before, let alone a black-and-white instant Polaroid.

I'm probably misquoting, but in *The Treasure of the Sierra Madre* an old man dances around, and Humphrey Bogart says, 'What are you dancing for?' – because they were looking for gold and Humphrey Bogart had been showing him rocks and other odd stones with what looks like traces of a coloured metal wedged in them, and the old man had said, 'No, that's just iron pyrites,' and thrown it away – then suddenly the old man, who has been gazing at the ground, is dancing – and Bogart, who is nearly at the end of his tether,

The Treasure of the Sierra Madre:
Walter Huston, Humphrey Bogart and Tim Holt

says, 'What are you dancing for and what are you so happy about?' And the old man says, 'You don't see the gold beneath your very feet' – the gold is in the mountain!

The old man has recognised something no one else can.

But it's more than that. We're bound by conventions, and it's astounding how we have to learn to see what is happening in front of our eyes. It's the classic thing of the train coming into the station – it was one of the very first films, made by the Lumière brothers – and as the train came hurtling towards the audience, they recoiled! Nowadays, they can't have enough explosions to make people jump in their seat.

I've always said there's not a right way and a wrong way.

There's a right way for the time and then there's another way, and I sense that we're at the end of the era when sound 'just' reflects the image – the end of hearing the match strike as it's going to light the candle. Sometimes we're not aware of the sound of the match striking because we're listening for something else. There's a scene in *Puffball* where Kelly Reilly wakes up in a hospital bed after she's had a Caesarean, and you hear the faint sound of the blinds banging against the window. But you soon become aware of a sound like a heartbeat underneath the sound of the blinds, which then takes over as Kelly moves out of the bed searching for her newborn child. The sound goes on until she reaches the baby in the next room.

Just as the storyteller in India didn't say anything about his objects – the dagger, the candle – as he was laying them out – he was talking about what a lovely day it was and 'This is a story I'm going to tell you,' but not about those objects – in the same way, I think we're scratching at the surface of the progress of sound.

You know, the loss of one of the senses is an extraordinary thing. When I was making *Don't Look Now* I went to see a recuperation centre for the blind. What was interesting was that part of the therapy and recuperation was a sort of blind theatre. Relatives and friends and members of the staff all turned up for a play the patients were putting on as part of their therapy. I thought, 'How are they going to do this?' I wanted to see it so that Hilary Mason, the actress who played the blind woman, could see their behaviour patterns, be among them and get a sense of their feelings and see how they moved about the stage.

The play took place in the sitting room of a country house, and they had doors in the back – sort of French windows – and furniture about the place, like a desk with a telephone on it. They knew their cues – when to come in. And the stage designer had put runners on the floor – carpet runners – to guide the actors. They couldn't see anything, but the runners were there to guide their bare feet to the desk or sofa. So the phone would ring and they'd go eight paces along the runners to the desk and pick up the phone. It was a marvellous way of familiarising them with the natural behaviour of people and helping them try and get over the absence of their sense of sight. A therapist once said to me that you find a lot of the loneliest people are the deaf. They become much more isolated in themselves. If you're blind, you can learn to read the sound of things, you can ask someone what they look like or whether something's blue – you can use your imagination. But the deaf have to make everything for themselves. Silence is extraordinarily isolating.

There's not much silence nowadays. Sound is around us all the time. Mobile phones – everyone's got their own attention-grabbing sound on their phone. We're becoming more attuned to people's sounds: we're listening in to people as they talk into their phones on buses or just walking down the street. Everybody is listening in to everybody 'for training purposes'! Consequently, people are becoming cautious about what they're saying, looking over their shoulder to see if anyone is listening. It reminds me of that marvellous

Americanism: 'You know what I'm saying?' And the reply: 'Yes, yes, I hear you, but *what* are you saying?' On *Puffball* I tried to push the boundaries of sound. Their conversation isn't really reflecting what their thoughts are; we hear their thoughts in another way.

Every telephone now has a camera in it. Years ago – probably when we were doing *Fahrenheit 451* – I remember someone saying, 'It'll be some time coming, but you'll have pictures on the phone,' and me thinking, 'Who would want that?' Now, everybody's got it – YouTube, I tube – everybody's got it, and it's happened so swiftly. Everyone is making images, and the 'commerce' of film – those who proclaim, 'Let them enjoy what we tell them' – is being defeated by this proliferation of images. There will always be this clash between corporate thought and the arts, and I can only hand on the baton now, but I love seeing what these young film-makers are now doing. I see how all our senses are up for investigation all the time and are changing. I had a line in *The Man Who Fell to Earth* and it really sums it up: 'The world is ever changing, Mr Farnsworth, like the universe.'

Script

Sitting between my two script-writers. Allan Scott on the right and
Chris Bryant, Allan's co-writer, on the left, in Venice 1971/2 on a location
recce for *Don't Look Now*. Sadly Chris died in 2008. Allan is still my great
good friend and collaborator.

The thought for a film begins either in reading a book or when something in your own life prompts a curious set of circumstances that you think might have some sort of story quality. Film is such a stepping stone that when you've finished, a whole section of your life has been taken up with it – beginning with the first thoughts and hopes and dreams, then the pre-production and the pre-pre-production, through the casting and then the financing – it all goes up and down, it's hardly smooth sailing.

At the end, it's taken up a lot of your life. In a way, it becomes your life.

A script is a very special form of writing. For me, it's a living thing, the first living component of what will become a motion picture. Which is quite exciting because it never stops. Sometimes scripts have taken five, six, ten years to be finally produced. The basic story elements are there, but the script must inevitably change because life changes, locations change, everything changes – dictated by the money and the finance.

Making a trailer is a wonderful way of studying film – and screenwriting. It's a very difficult art form. I once worked with a couple of American trailer-makers who lived in England,

and the difference, at that time, between a studio-made trailer and an independent one was huge. A good trailer should get to the essence of the story – not just the action, not just the sex scene or the other obvious things. It should present the intrigue and strangeness and excitement of the film. It doesn't necessarily just focus on a moment in the film that's remembered for all time – a great moment as in *Lawrence of Arabia*, when Omar Sharif comes out of the desert. That's not necessarily good for the trailer because it creates a sort of disappointment about what the film actually is.

Trailer-making is a very odd but marvellous art form. It would be great to find some old trailer and look at the film and see if the trailer captures the essence of that film. It's difficult when it's not an action film, when it's a film that relies on performance – because some moments of a performance can look corny if taken out of context.

There was a young writer/director I admired. I liked his short and thought he was doing something rather interesting with film. We spoke and he wanted to come and have a chat about his work, and then he said, 'I'm finishing off a script. Do you mind if I pop it round to you – would you read it?'

I hate doing that because I'm not a teacher, but he's a very nice guy and so I said, 'Bring it round, but I'm not going to criticise it – we'll talk about something in it.' So about three or four weeks later he popped it round, and I read it. It was really quite long, but at first I thought, 'God, this is very, very carefully covered.' It was rather like a release script, which is something that the studios send out if they're in competition for a festival or sometimes send for a foreign version of the film, so that everything is described. It's very different from the original script because the people who make the release script type it out from the completed film, so every shot – 'Cut to Close-up', etc. – is in it. If one wrote a script that was that accurate to the final film it would be a miracle; in fact, it would be impossible – things just change on the floor.

So I started reading his script. Everything was very carefully described – he must have been making the movie in his head, virtually shot by shot – nothing was generalised. I'd never read anything quite like it because it was so completely covered – no room for any change, no room for anything at all. It was practically dictated, just like a release script typed from the completed film.

I spoke to him about it and said, 'It's very difficult for me to make a comment on it. I'll help you, I'll talk to someone about it. I'm not saying that it's something I would like to do, I'm not saying that. I think it would be difficult for anyone else to direct it because it's so complete in itself. I can't imagine any other way for it to go now because that's the film! I'll help you meet someone else – it's very difficult for me to recommend it – but I'll just tell them it's very cleverly done and very well covered, if they like the subject and they like the attitude in it, but there isn't any room for development.'

Inevitably, he'll have to direct it himself, but when he starts shooting it, he'll find it'll change its shape and its form – its scenes and its look will change. That's what screenwriters find when they do it themselves, a screenwriter directing his own piece – he finds he changes it too.

It's just not over till it's over – a film is being made right to the end. I often laugh that they have to tear the film away from me – even with the DVD version: 'Don't let him touch it any more.' Just like your life, it changes from minute to minute and the things that you'd imagined would happen don't.

In the main, a script is always an unfinished work. It will almost certainly change – the locations change, when you get to the art department they will interpret it differently – and that's where the director is like a jockey: he listens to the interpretation of the art department and says, 'That's not a bad way to go, but I'd prefer it to be . . . However, we'll try and fit with those thoughts.' Then the cinematographer interprets the look that should be on the screen and discusses it – 'Is it low-key, is it dark, do we . . .?'

I was the cinematographer on *A Funny Thing Happened on the Way to the Forum*, which had been a musical play on Broadway set in ancient Rome with Zero Mostel. It had mystery in it, but a humorous kind of mystery. There was a scene with Mostel creeping upstairs at night. The scene was described as 'night-time, a dangerous place to be' – but, of course, you can't photograph it like that. It was a comedy and so you could only give an impression of night-time, an impression of the dark and the shadows on the stairs, because you have to see their faces to get the joke – you have to see Zero Mostel looking round the corner. It would be impossible if it were shot like a mystery and there's a shadow across his face – the scene relies on the comical attitude his face expressed. 'Night-time, a dangerous place to be' – you can't really dictate that with a script.

I don't like working on a script on my own. I don't even like discussing a script on my own very much – except in the broadest terms. I want someone else there – obviously someone with talent or ability, or someone whose work I admire.

People send me scripts asking if I might be interested in them. If I'm caught by the script, if it's got a premise that hooks me, I usually ask what the source material is or if it is an original, then I want to meet the writer. I want to talk to the writer because then, if I like it and it goes forward, it becomes an adaptation of the original, not page by page: 'It says here: "She got up and went down to the kitchen for a while."' That's not what I want – I want to see what the truth of it is. It might change completely in terms of the location or even what the character does – if I can see there's a running truth in it.

I'll never forget Daphne du Maurier on *Don't Look Now*: after the film was shot, du Maurier asked to see it and the producer said, 'Oh, Nic, you'd better not come because you've changed it so much and we don't want any trouble with her saying anything to the press.' And I said, 'I haven't changed it – I've changed some detail, but not the heart of the piece.' And he said, 'Still, you'd better not come! We're having a private screening for her – and I think also one of her daughters.'

After the screening the producer phoned me and said, 'I think it went all right, she didn't say much.'

About a week or ten days later I had a very nice letter from her and she said something like: 'Dear Mr Roeg, Last week I saw your film of my story. Your John and Laura reminded me so much of the young couple I saw once on Torcello. They looked still very much in love, but with a terrible problem . . .' and she went on to talk about it.

In the book, after the child's death, John and Laura go on holiday to Venice – but I gave John the job of restoring a church there. I thought Venice is such a wonderful, extraordinary place, and for them just to go on holiday there didn't feel right. I was making up ideas for the story in my own head, but I didn't betray her story at all. She was a real writer, a storyteller.

In India, the storytellers carry around with them their stories of myth and extraordinariness. Some are better storytellers than others, but it's the same basic story . . . the story of life.

I feel very much with film that you have to cast the writer as you would cast an actor. On one occasion, I was working on something for Dino De Laurentiis, and he wanted me to use a certain writer. We met and we talked about the subject, and I told him what my feelings were and he said what he liked about it – which were all valid things, and I wasn't being judgemental about him – but I thought, 'We're not thinking of it in quite the same way.' I liked him and he was a nice guy and he obviously had a lot of good credits. We had meetings and went backwards and forwards for about ten days. Finally, I said, 'I don't think it's going to work,' and he said, 'I don't think so either – we're just off kilter.' We talked to the producer, and the writer said to the producer, 'The problem is I give Nic six ideas and he rejects seven of them!' I loved that . . . If only he'd been thinking in this wild way when we were working together.

I was involved for some time with *Out of Africa*, the novel by Karen Blixen, who wrote under the name of Isak Dinesen. There was a wonderful young American writer, Judith Rascoe, and we worked together on the screenplay. Si Litvinoff was going to produce it – he'd got some development money – and we went off to Denmark. Obviously, by this time Dinesen was dead, so we went to Copenhagen to talk to her estate. People had tried to film *Out of Africa* before, they'd written scripts, but the estate didn't want it to be a sensational film because Isak Dinesen was a national treasure in Denmark – so they guarded her work and had never given their permission. Our script was the first one that was given the approval of the Isak Dinesen estate. Clara Svendsen had been her secretary and was involved with running the estate; she had to be the first to read it because she and Dinesen had been very close. She read it – and for a few days we heard nothing – then we had a message that she wanted to meet me and talk about the script and the story and what I'd thought of Dinesen's life – and especially her relationship with Denys Finch Hatton, who was the great love of her life. They were lovers, but it wasn't the accepted thing – I don't think she was divorced from her husband, she was very much a Danish aristo. Finch Hatton was killed in an airplane crash. He was a pilot and flew his light aircraft around Africa – funnily enough, he crashed on his way back to see Dinesen.

So Clara Svendsen said, 'Yes, I'd like to give permission. I shall be voting at the trustee meeting – I think it would be good to go ahead with it. You have our blessing.' We were thrilled. The next day we were having a drink together at the hotel and she said a strange thing to me: 'I was looking at your script again last night, and it made me remember when I was sitting with Isak in her study one evening and I said to her, "Is everything all right, Isak? You look worried." And she said, "Yes, I was just thinking about Denys, and that it would have been so much easier for me when he was killed if I'd been able to wear black." What she meant was, to be able to openly mourn her lover. I always thought it was a marvellous thing: 'It would have been so much easier if when he was killed I'd been able to wear black. I could openly mourn him.' And coming from Clara Svendsen – I thought, 'My God, we've touched a truth.' Judith and I had touched on a truth in our script.

But life went on, and eventually we didn't make the film. I'd said to one of the heads of the studio, 'We *are* going to do this, aren't we?' And he'd said, 'Yes, Nic, Yes, Nic, Yes, Nic. That's three times, I can't say more. Does that satisfy you?' That was in his office one morning and we went off to lunch, very happy, but they didn't do it. The studio got taken over and things went into 'turnaround' and we lost the rights – which were picked up by other people. So, what can you do?

Over my career, I've been involved in many, many books,

and a particular one I liked very much was a story from a collection by Lillian Hellman that was called *Pentimento*. The story was called *Julia*. It came to me quite by chance and I really liked it – it was set during the beginning of the Nazi rise to power in Germany. We got a bit underway with it – I went to see Jane Fonda and she liked the idea of it. Lillian Hellman was terrific. I wasn't working with her on it, but I had a terrific rapport with her. But somewhere along the line, Harold Pinter became involved.

Harold was going through a bit of a crisis in his life at the time, but we became quite close while we were working on it – he also liked the story, the idea of it, and I thought we were progressing well. Tragically, things came to a crisis with Harold. I didn't realise what was happening in his private life – and it was none of my business anyway. We'd met and had long talks – we'd done a few pages, and he'd done some outlines and things. But the studio people wanted to know how we were getting on. I had to fly out to California to let them know because we were running very behind with the script – we'd done, at most, twenty or thirty pages, but we had notes and notes and notes – a joint exchange of all our chats and meetings.

I tried to reach Harold before leaving, I wanted to tell him I was on my way, maybe he could fly out as well, but I hadn't been able to get in touch with him. I thought: 'Oh well, he's very busy now.' So I went off to California and two days later I had to go into this big meeting, and they said, 'How's it going, Nic? What's happening? How's Harold? Is he happy?'

I said, 'Yes, it's fantastic, we've got some fantastic scenes' – winging it, as they say. Outlining it, telling them about our notes, but making them sound like scenes. They were very excited.

I got back from the meeting and thought, 'I've got to reach Harold – this is crazy' – and I phoned from California. I remember his secretary answered and said, 'Oh Nic, he's not here now.' I said, 'It's very, very important I speak to him, I'm getting nervous because I can't reach him. I've just had a meeting and I know he'd want . . .' But she said, 'I'll let him know. Maybe if you call tomorrow . . .'

I thought: 'There's something wrong here,' so I phoned straight back on another number I had and Harold picked up the phone and said, 'Hello.'

His secretary hadn't fobbed me off well enough!

I said, 'Harold, what's up?'

He said, 'I'm going to have to get in touch with the agents because I can't go on with it, Nic.'

I said, 'What!'

Harold: 'I can't.'

Nic: 'I've just told them how great it is! How we're full steam ahead.'

Anyway, it was disastrous and the film fell apart. But the weirdest thing is that it began in a curious way – it began with a producer named Roth. I was staying at the Beverley Hills Hotel while working on something else and there was a note slipped under my door saying: There's a gentleman in the lobby who would love to see you and if we put him through would you accept the call?

I said, 'OK' – they put me through and he said, 'I'm leaving a book for you to read' – it was *Pentimento*. He said, 'There's a story in it I'd like you to make.' I thanked him and he asked how long I was staying – I said about a week and he said, 'It's only a short story, but if you could read it before you leave . . .' I read it and thought it was terrific, it hit me immediately – it was *Julia*. He phoned a couple of days later and we met, talked about it – how strange and marvellous it was – and as he was leaving, I said: 'You do own it. I mean, you're not . . .' He said, 'Of course, I own it.'

The upshot was he didn't own it. So, in a curious way, the thing wasn't destined for me – Fred Zinnemann did it in the end. The best thing that came out of it was actually meeting Lillian Hellman. I met her in New York; I'd loved Dashiel Hammett with whom she had lived – an extraordinary romantic relationship – tough and goodness knows what. We went out to dinner a few times – she had an extraordinary attitude, she could also sink a few, scotches and such. We went back to her apartment – there was a photograph of Hammett on the desk – and as I was leaving the apartment she said – I'll never forget it – she said, 'You know, I think we'll get along great because I like the way you know the difference between "perhaps" and "maybe".'

It was beautiful – it stuck in my head. It's such a marvellous thought. I've had the word 'maybe' come up in scripts at times – in fact, there's a moment in *Don't Look Now* where I decided to change it to 'perhaps' – it's a word with that smell of difference in it.

Scripts are very curious things. I mean, they very rarely

– I can't stress this enough – reflect what is the final movie. Very rarely, certainly in my experience.

Inevitably, it's a different medium. The script says, 'Battle Scene – the soldiers come over the hill and charge down the hill.' That's a line and a half. But it takes a week to shoot it. Over the course of that week, things happen – inevitably, so much changes – even the form of heroism the hero takes.

With the coming of sound, the studios sent people across the country, from the West Coast to the East Coast, to get writers – playwrights and novelists. I've been in situations where I've been offered scripts written by the author of the novel – and sometimes a scriptwriter is involved as well. And usually the script is too literary. By that I mean the words are used to tell everything: 'He looks at her with disbelief in his face' – but how he looks at her needs to be built up from within the scene, not dictated by words. Film can be much more of a reality than a page with words can ever be. You cannot compare a film with a book.

In the end, it's about truth – staying true to the truth inside the book. The premise of the piece, the truth of it, belongs to the author – but the form is different. I've done two films adapted from books, and, fortunately, both authors have liked what I've done. With *Puffball*, Fay Weldon liked it because the way I handled the death of the child was true to the book. With *Don't Look Now*, in the book the child didn't die of drowning, it was meningitis. The truth is the death of the child, not the way it happens.

I read a little book called *Walkabout*, which was about two kids lost in the Australian desert. It opened lots of doors in my head about lost children. I'd just been to see a play at the Royal Court by Edward Bond. I wrote to him about *Walkabout*, and had a note back from him saying he liked the idea, especially as he had been thinking about writing a play about a journey – that really hooked me, and I said that I also liked the idea of a story about a journey. The journey would be the plot. He said, 'Why don't I try something?' Then, about three weeks later: 'I think I've got it, Nic. I've got a draft.' And he sent me fourteen pages.

It was fantastic. The scenes were alive, beautifully alive. They were stripped down to the most beautiful single moments. There was one point where the little boy and the girl are walking up this hill, and they get to the top and the boy is standing on the ridge and looks out across the landscape and sees this great shimmering thing – he thinks it's the sea, though in fact it's a mirage. The little boy is happy and excited, and he points to the mirage and says, 'Look. There's the sea.' And his sister, who is sixteen, says, 'Maybe.' He responds, 'It's the sea.' But he sees that she is not excited and he says, 'It is the sea, isn't it?' And she says, 'Perhaps.' And they walk on. Imagine those three phrases – 'There's the sea,' 'It's the sea,' 'It is the sea, isn't it?' – a few words said in different ways, but the same words. Containing all the emotions. And the doubt too. It's so filmic – just the dialogue without any description of the emotion to be expressed through the dialogue. It was so spare, but truthful, without trying to explain the various emotions the boy was going through. In these few words the child goes through all these different attitudes, without the script giving any information in terms

Walkabout: Luc Roeg and Jenny Agutter

of literary description, without dressing it up with bits in between like: 'The sky was getting dark like bruises on a virgin's arms.' It had a kind of nakedness – all the rest I, as the director, would fill in.

The last time I saw Edward Bond was at his agent's office.

Later that afternoon I was due to meet one of the executives of the British division of the American production company that was putting up the money for the film. I'd delivered the fourteen-page first draft and I'd heard on the grapevine that they were very upset and very anxious about it and wanted to see me. I'd heard that Edward was going to be in town that afternoon, so I said I'd go see the producers afterwards. Edward was in a kind of conference room – he was standing with his back to the door, looking out of the window – and I said, 'I've just popped by to say the script's terrific, I love it. It was really good working with you.' I knew I could shoot it. I said to him, 'Would you like to come to Australia?' He said, 'No, no, no, I don't want to go – you do all that, Nic.' I looked at my watch and said, 'I've got to go to this meeting with the production company,' and he said, 'Goodbye.' He still had his back to me, looking out of the window – I can see it now. And he said, 'I think it's the best thing I've ever done.' That was the last time I saw him.

Later on that afternoon I went to the meeting with the producer, and he said, 'Nic, I can't send this to America – it's fourteen pages of:

ABO: Xxx.
BOY: Where?
ABO: Xxx.

'What is this? You'll have to get me off the hook – you know I'm behind you on this, but I'm going to be fired.' So I actually had to write a letter saying that 'I realise why you feel that way, but these fourteen pages are just the skeleton of the piece' – and I filled in a lot of 'dressing' to go with it. I just wrote things like: 'They stumbled through a lava field that seemed to be dragging them into a different . . .' – just so that it filled out to about fifty, sixty pages, which they said made it just about feasible to be made. The actual basic thread of the film was only fourteen pages, but you can't always see the beauty on the page. It's very difficult. You can't read the emotion. That can only be done in the performance.

Jeffrey Eugenides, the American author of *The Virgin Suicides*, wrote this about *Walkabout* for an article about summer movies for *The New Yorker*:

Thinking about summer movies, I find myself returning not to a first-run cinema rumbling with some blockbuster's rigged detonations but to the ballroom of our old yacht club in Detroit. In that vast, velvet-draped space, whenever a boozy regatta party didn't intervene, movies were shown. One July evening, my mother and I ended up at an Australian film we knew nothing about beyond its mystifying title: *Walkabout*.

Summer explained why we were alone together. My oldest brother, a folk musician, worked nights. My father and my other brother were racing our sailboat up to Mackinac. And so my mother and I got into her car – which used to be my father's until it got old and temperamental – and made the long drive into the city.

'The oil light's on,' I said, as we were crossing the Belle Isle bridge.

'It does that,' my mother said.

The film began unthreateningly. A father drives his children, a teenage daughter and young son, into the outback. At first, all seems

Walkabout: David Gulpilil, Luc Roeg and Jenny Agutter

well. They picnic. The sister and brother go for a walk. Suddenly, the father fires a gun in their direction. Hiding behind a rock, the girl looks back to see her father dowsing the car with gasoline. In the next second, he immolates the vehicle, along with himself.

Lost in the wilderness, the girl and boy are doomed. But fate intervenes: they meet an Aborigine who is in the midst of the test of manhood known as the walkabout. He hunts game for them and teaches them how to siphon water from the ground. The parched, lizard-ridden landscape becomes lush as they journey. Soon the Aborigine and the girl are cavorting naked in an oasis. Later, as they near civilization, the Aborigine performs a mating dance, to which the girl doesn't respond, and the next morning she finds that he has hanged himself in a tree.

Two suicides. A lengthy montage of Edenic, but fully frontal, nudity. And all without my mother putting her hand over my eyes. Beyond the wondrous excitement of all this was the message the film conveyed, and for which there existed no better recipient than

73

a twelve-year-old growing up in the wake of the sixties: civilization was evil, technology deracinating, and the only solution a return to nature. I'd had a glimpse into a world of adult seriousness, in which fathers despaired of their lives and children, abandoned, had to fend for themselves.

As we went to our car, my mother and I made appreciative noises about the film in order to disguise the awkwardness of having seen it together. It must have been clear to my mother that she was losing me to all the film depicted, not only to sexuality but to a life without a parental center. The film's suggestion, that a father wasn't something to be counted on, we left unvoiced, but that general idea – of the irrelevancy of fathers – always hovered between a mother and son.

Further exploiting my father's absence, I rolled down my window. He would never have allowed that – not in the city at night. My father would have secured the doors and windows and turned the air-conditioning on full blast. My mother was too busy to notice. The red oil light had flashed on again. I watched her frowning at it, then turned back to the window.

In the reeds along the river, radios were playing. People were lying on blankets in the grass, or dancing together in the gazebos, bottles glinting in their hands.

I was older than I'd been two hours earlier. I was ready to get out of the car right then and there. I could wander into the woods of Belle Isle, go back over the bridge, past the Chrysler factory, all the way downtown. Over to Canada, even. Or south to Toledo. Or at least to college someday. Wherever my walkabout would take me.

'I'll tell you one thing,' my mother said, rapping her knuckles against the oil light. 'I'm about ready to set this car on fire.'

We had a good laugh over that. Outside, I could smell the river, the blowsy cattails, the throat-coating, Kaopectate wind from the cement factory on the opposite shore.

Like Jeffrey Eugenides, Jenny Agutter was also older by the time the film was finished: she was sixteen when we began and turned seventeen during the shoot – from a girl into a woman. My son Luc went on a similar journey – curious about everything, fearing nothing. And for myself, making the film was also a journey: we didn't have a location manager, we simply got into the trucks each day and drove till we found a location I felt was right for the film. We found the film as we made it.

When Edward Bond gave me the script he said there weren't very many words. 'Words are for the theatre. You're the director, you provide the rest.'

I became very friendly with the author Paul Theroux, whose work I admired. On meeting him, I found that his views on film reflected so much and so closely what I felt about movie storytelling – its ability to leap backwards and forwards in time, making it more visually accurate than could possibly be done with words alone. I think his letter printed here brilliantly describes the difference between writing a book and writing a movie. Script discussion becomes open to almost everyone – you don't have to be a grammarian or follow any established set of rules or construction. I think his letter says everything about the difference between how the story of a novel grows and how the script of a movie only lays the foundation and hints at what the final film will really be about.

After we spoke, while I was in London, I sent you an email, but probably to the wrong address, since I haven't heard back. So here I am writing an old-fashioned letter.

I just wanted to say that I look forward to reading your book. Perhaps you've already discovered the strange simplicity of book-writing. You write a page, you improve it, and there it is. When you have a stack it's a narrative; when you have a bigger stack it's a book. You do it alone.

So different from script -writing: months of pondering, talking, arguing, writing, rewriting, hoping like hell, intense work, passion...and what happens? I recall the months, perhaps years, of *The Dead Girls* and years of *Chicago Loop* scripts. All that work we did with hope and the passage of time – and with what results? Rejection, oblivion. You could tell the same story a hundred times over. As Shakespeare said in a sonnet, 'When in the chronicle of wasted time . . . They had not skill enough your worth to sing; For we, which now behold these present days, Have eyes to wonder, but lack tongues to praise.'

By all means please share my letter with your editor, and feel free to use it. I was just spinning my wheels, thinking about script-writing. Movie-making itself (unlike script-writing) seems to me to have a great deal of enjoyment built into it, like a carnival rolling into town and taking over – and you, as director, have the best seat – like a puppet master, captain of the ship, circus leader. Making a film is creating a whole world – I mean physically doing it. Not to be compared with a schmuck with a typewriter. I love the idea of one of my books being made into a film, since a film is a completely different form; and I laugh when writers complain about how their book got ruined etc. My complaint is that not enough good books get made into films. There are at the moment options on five of my books. I pray that they get made! You have a genuine love of reading and a liking for writers. John Huston also had it; not many others.

In the course of our script-writing sessions you shared a great deal of your early life, your father's age (and remarriage); your country house being plundered by robbers with a van; your reckless, impulsive, utterly necessary love affairs . . . one of them with you naked in a hotel room with a famous actress and her crazed suitor outside banging on the door pleading in a romantic way, 'Please let's talk . . . I respect you so much!' . . . Your requirement for passion: 'strange skin'. On a hotel guest register in the space where profession/occupation was to be entered you wrote "Gentleman" and then out-gazed the clerk as he read it and looked up at you for a moment and then decided not to question it. I think that was in Samoa, wasn't it? Yes, I have a good memory. Please include some of this.

I look forward to reading whatever you write about life, love, the past, the future, creativity, work, and whether anything really matters.

One thing I must add to Paul's letter. After some time trying to float the *Chicago Loop* script, Paul had the idea of reversing the usual procedure of writing a book and then selling the movie rights and writing the script. He said he was fed up with all the explanations and meetings, he said he'd write the book of the script and sell an option on it to write the script! He wrote the book and it won the New York best book of the month, or some such award. Options were picked up, but again after readings and more meetings it still didn't go any further and the options were gradually dropped.

I have a nice copy of the book, with a nice dedication. Value and worth in any of the arts has always been about timing. Something is so often 'after its time' or 'before'. Of

the two it is more likely to be given a green light if it's 'after its time' (it can be understood as a 'period piece'). Who knows anything about the future 'before its time'? *Chicago Loop* has lived through both.

Directing

With Donald Cammell (on my left) and a visitor
outside the house on Powis Square on *Performance*

Making a movie is like making a marvellous soup. The actors, the cameraman, the editor, writer, producer, technicians – everyone, they're all in this soup. But the taster of the soup is the director. Of course, there are so many fundamental jobs involved in making a film, so many creative people – and you need their help and friendship in developing your thoughts for the film into a unified whole. But it's the director who says, 'It needs more salt.' So, as a director, you're in a very lonely place because you can't be entirely truthful about things. Sometimes you let things go, despite what you feel. Sometimes you're shooting something, and during the take you decide that you don't really need that close-up, but you let it go on and say 'Print it' at the end just for the sake of morale.

The loneliness of the director – it reminds me of when I had come to the end of my work on *Lawrence of Arabia* in Morocco. It was pretty much the end of the movie as well. I was with David Lean in his caravan; we were doing a pick-up shot or something – I can't remember exactly why it was just my camera crew – and gradually people were packing up and coming by the caravan, saying goodbye to him. All the location cars were picking up people, and everybody was relaxed.

It was a massive unit, and they gradually disappeared. The film was over.

I looked out of the caravan and saw my operator, Alex Thompson, who later became a great cameraman, pacing around in the desert. He looked over and was tapping his watch – he wanted to get in the car and for us both to leave. I looked at David, who was sitting obviously deep in thought. I said, 'I've got to go now, David,' and he said, 'Oh yes, yes, that's OK, Nic, that's OK.' I left the caravan and looked back, and he was standing in the doorway. My car wasn't far from the caravan, and he stepped down and moved off on his own. Virtually the last trucks and cars were leaving, but he was completely lost in thought. I said to Alex, 'Hold on a minute.' David came quite close to the car, but he didn't look at it at all. He had tears in his eyes. I watched him go by, and he walked off towards some dunes. My last image of him is him standing on the dunes with his back to me, just looking out at the desert.

This image of Lean alone reminds me of something that John Huston wrote. I think he said somewhere that when you're making a movie – especially a movie the size of *Lawrence* – first of all you get the script, you get the money and goodness knows what, and then pre-production starts and people start inhabiting the offices – and I say 'inhabiting' because it becomes rather like a small town and the director is its mayor. Gradually people arrive and sets are built and everyone comes to talk to the mayor. Then the movie starts and the actors arrive. It's a thriving town and everybody's working; it's a full town, rather like a gold rush – you know, the town flourishes as long as the gold's there. Gradually the film comes to a close. The gold's gone, the people have deserted the village, and the director is the last person to leave that village. The last shops have closed and the houses are up for sale, and maybe the town's going to be erased from the Earth. Huston said at the end of his piece, which was a kind of reminiscence on directing: 'Taken all in all, it's rather a melancholy affair.' I think that's right: those great highs are followed by an emptiness that is quite extraordinary – a whole slice of life has come to an end. People you've been very intimate with – you see them again because crews seem to crop up again, but some will have gone on to something else – you can't have the same crew all the time – so life is divided up in movies. And the intensity of that and all the associations and hopes and dreams . . . it's a very melancholy affair.

I don't like anybody – assistant director or not – expecting or knowing exactly when the cut comes. Only *I* say 'cut' – it's a cardinal rule. I remember when I was photographing *Fahrenheit 451*, François Truffaut didn't like anybody to say 'cut'; he liked scenes to come to their natural end. We had a scene where the firemen arrive at an old lady's house. At least Montag (Oskar Werner) *thinks* it's the old lady's house, but then he realises that it's his house: 'What's going on?' And that was supposed to be the shot: Montag realising that his house is going to be searched for contraband books as the fire truck pulls up to his house. So the fire truck drives up and the shot had sort of run out, and Oskar asked, 'Is this shot over or are we continuing? What's happening?' But

François Truffaut (in the middle) on the set of *Fahrenheit 451*
with Oscar Werner on the right

François just went 'Shhhh' as the camera moved forward – and suddenly one of the other firemen laughed. And François said, 'Cut!' He didn't explain anything. And later, when we were in the cutting room, François cut in the laugh. It was perfect because it came from the fireman who was jealous of Montag. It wasn't in the script – it came from the mistaken, unrehearsed moment.

I hardly rehearse scenes. I discuss them, but when the time comes to shoot the scene, I've moved on; it becomes too set. Say you arrive on location and you have planned to have a young, loving couple say goodbye in the sunshine on the beach, and as the girl walks away you see her shadow growing longer as the sun sets. All this is described in the script. And then you arrive there and it's raining. The production people say, 'Let's go back to the studio. Leave the scene.' I say, 'No. Bring out the camera, set up, and we'll shoot the scene.' But instead of saying goodbye in the sunshine and shadows and dropping sun, it's raining. As the girl walks away you see rain on her cheeks, like tears running down. The scene still has its own impetus. So I don't do rehearsals, though I may shoot a scene two or three times for different reasons. I hate rehearsals – that's something left over from the theatre.

I'm not sure if it's apocryphal or not, that scene between Brando and Rod Steiger in *On the Waterfront* – Brando forgot his lines or something, so he made it up. It's one of the great scenes in the movie – and the director, Elia

With François Truffaut and his assistant

85

Kazan, recognised that. It wasn't Brando's form to do endless rehearsals; he wanted to 'seize the moment'. People forget their lines in films – and suddenly the performance changes. They forget the line and their face changes, and it's a fantastic expression because you can see on their face that something's gone out of their mind. If you rehearse too much, you miss these kinds of moments.

Sometimes I'll say 'Turn over' to the cameraman while the actors are waiting for me to say 'Action', thinking that it might be interesting to have them just talking, people just talking: what are they talking about – who knows? You know, sometimes if you stick too closely to what you've thought of the night before, you miss the beauty of the moment. Similarly, once a scene's under way, I like it if it runs on – you're all caught up in it and the actors have come to the end of what's been rehearsed and, suddenly, for that moment as they think, 'Are we going a line further?' they just blurt something out or do something unexpected. Or actors sometimes do something by mistake during a scene – they catch their arm on a hook or something – and that changes the whole quality of the scene from what they had intended in their head. Like Walter Huston says in *The Treasure of the Sierra Madre*: 'You don't see the gold beneath your very feet. It's right here in the most unlikely place.' So that's why I never let anyone say 'Cut' on the set. For me, chance and coincidence are really exciting, but you can't really relax into chance and coincidence if you're driving on something you've already prepared.

A film set is a wonderful workplace. Everyone is part of

the movie: the prop man, the electricians, the wardrobe, the costume designer, the carpenters – they're all part of the movie and all this work is an offering to the film. The production designer is especially important. The art department is a very curious thing – it covers pretty well everything: script and set and building and locations and costumes, because it all goes together with the picture. The production designer, who used to be just called the art director, is really worth listening to about a lot of things because he's searching for a truth in everything. All things are connected. His responsibility is to all those sections of the art department. When people say, 'Beautifully designed . . . what a great look it had,' but then add, 'But I didn't like the movie,' then something hasn't married. There's something odd about that. It's the absurdity of awards: the art direction got the award, but the movie wasn't very good. But it's part of the whole, you can't divorce it. The movie either works or it doesn't – you have to think of it as a whole. I don't think you can have a great movie where the art direction doesn't work – it belongs to it.

The whole idea of the production designer has advanced tremendously and broadened its scope because of the idea that you can shoot on location. You can find the natural location for most things – except in great sci-fi epics, but even then, because of CGI now, you can marry extraordinary images seamlessly, which at one time you couldn't. In the old days, going on location was a big event – for financial reasons, more than anything else.

There's that marvellous old expression: 'A rock is a rock,

a tree is a tree, so let's shoot it in Griffith Park!' Don't let's bother with even thinking about going on location because one shot in one place looks exactly like another – one sand dune looks like another. Even with *Walkabout* we were thinking of doing a couple of pick-up shots with sand dunes just outside LA. With *Doctor Zhivago*, we were waiting for snow, and when we didn't get it in Moscow we made do with artificial snow. The charge of the Cossacks was shot with whirlwinds built up with artificial snow.

The whole idea behind everything is the image. The image is the art. It either conveys the feeling or it doesn't, so it can be natural or artificial. At one time everything was shot in the studio because photographing a film on location was technically very difficult – you needed generators for lamps – so it was cheaper and easier for the production designer to make a garden. The studios had the gardening department, so it was: 'Send for the gardeners. These flowers need replacing.' And they'd go out to another section of the studio and come back with a trolley of flowers. 'We can make it springtime overnight, but it'll take at least this evening to get it done. When can we come in and put the buds on the trees? What time will you be finishing on the set?'

The production designer really did build things – like a beautifully built set with an extraordinary garden. And these sets would be kept to be used again. The garden scene might be quite a short scene, but the production designer would have built it so that the director could make the choice of how he would shoot the scene, and probably a lot of the set wasn't even seen – it was in the distance or shown from one angle. Everything is completely different if you change the angle, so no one would recognise the reverse angle of the garden if they put it in another movie, so they used to keep sets.

So the whole technical side of art direction was very different from now, where location shooting is much more the norm. That old Gary Cooper film, *Beau Geste*, was set in the Moroccan desert, but it was shot in Los Angeles. Hollywood recreated the famous London fog with their fog machines, they laid on noise soundtracks – the hooting of automobile horns, the sound of policemen's footsteps coming out of this mist. I remember shooting these kinds of scenes in artificial mist and fog – it was really exciting.

The Hollywood studios had big warehouses they called 'stages' – 'We're shooting on Stage 7.' That word came from the fact that – it's almost impossible to believe – in the early days of silent movies they actually built a stage – a proper theatre stage – in an exterior, with sides and wings. And they would swivel this stage so that the sun could hit it in the correct way. D. W. Griffith was avant-garde, in a way. He said, 'We could shoot it on a horse! We could stand on the ground and shoot it! We don't need a stage any more.' That kind of attitude – it's fantastic. 'Let's shoot it in a more natural way.' Nowadays it's difficult to tell whether it's artificial or not, it's so brilliantly done. But before technology took over, it was the production designer who was responsible for the balance between reality and invention. It's always marvellous working with a clever production designer.

There was one I really liked called Richard Macdonald –

he did *Far from the Madding Crowd*. We had long discussions and many arguments about things, but the production designer and the cameraman are always at loggerheads. It's rather like having someone who is continually advising you what you should wear or what you should eat. The production designer and the cameraman are both after the same end, but come at it from a different point of view.

There was a wonderful production designer at MGM, Alfred Junge. He thought everybody but the art department was stupid. I forget what movie it was on, but I was the assistant to Freddie Young, who was a brilliant, brilliant cameraman. Freddie was starting to light the set, and he was changing the power of the lamp from 2K. He said to me, 'Tell the electricians to put a 10K on there – I can't believe it's still dark in that corner.' So he went over to the end of the set, and found that Junge had painted in the shadows where he thought they should be painted! Shadows on the set! God! There was a tremendous clash – I've never heard such screaming and things! It was extraordinary – where to put the lamp or where not to put the lamp – 'In case you didn't realise, as the light goes down there's a great shadow passing, so I've shown you where the shadow should be.' Junge was trying to show Freddie how it should look. It was a perfect example of the production designer and the cameraman being at odds.

John Box was another tremendously interesting production designer – he did *Zhivago* and *Lawrence*, as well as a lot of other very interesting work. Production designers need to know something about the actual technical restraints on lighting a set, so he said to me, 'Have a look at these designs.' He'd provided for what we called a 'floating ceiling', which you could take out and put back to cope with the lighting rig, and it was just at the time when, from a photographic point of view, things were changing as far as the equipment and lighting were concerned – the look of the film and the story was changing in terms of the photography. And I remember him saying, 'We could allow you a tracking shot between the two sets – I've made a knife edge.' A knife-edge set comes to a very fine point so that as you track along outside it, it practically dissolves from one room to another – for instance, tracking alongside a secretary as she's walking through doors – an old-fashioned technique, which was interesting for some things. And I said, 'John, it would be really exciting for me if you made it more difficult for me, because difficulty always inspires you – doesn't it?' You think, "How will I do this?" instead of, "Oh yes, I know how to do this." And you revert to the normal thing of a back light and a front light and a filler light. But if you can't get a back light in, then you have to think, "Maybe we should expose something..."' And I remember him saying, 'That's the first time in my life I've been asked by the cameraman to make it more difficult for him to shoot a scene.'

Maybe I was being perverse – but then the cameraman is always trying to interpret the story. Although the director has the final say, it doesn't diminish the wonderful world of the production designer.

Location managers are also part of the art department. There's a marvellous place in America – Monument Valley, some way outside Los Angeles on the Utah–Arizona border, where they shot a lot of Westerns. It's just superb, every view of it. There are some iconic pillars of stone and sandstone that you'd recognise from one film to another. When you go to Monument Valley, it's like going to a giant film set. They have signposts pointing out the spot where the stagecoach went by in that great John Ford western with John Wayne. It's got little plaques that say, 'On this spot such and such a scene happened.' I think that's an extraordinarily exciting thing for movies. These locations have become classic in the same way as 'This is the place where the Great Fire of London blazed' at the Monument in the City. When the location manager stumbled across the most extraordinary scenery in Monument Valley, he must have gone back to the studio and said, 'I think I've found the right place. We could shoot a hundred and fifty movies here!' It's perfect. From every angle, the view is different. Beautiful and great and huge.

I once had a cottage in the country that had a beautiful view – it truly was 'where every prospect pleases – and only man is vile' – except me, I'm not vile! We had a watercolour society in the village, and they would come down and say, 'Do you mind if we use your field? We'll set up our canvases and our easels . . .' I watched them go down to the field, and they'd set up a canvas and then they'd look and shift the canvas to one side and then shift it another way – 'Do you like that view? Ah, yes, that's the view we like.' Well, to me that isn't being inspired by the look of something. I have a rule on set – it probably annoys a lot of people: once it's dressed, once it's started to be played in don't touch anything, don't clean anything. Don't touch anything because that becomes the truth of the set, and if the camera ends up with a shot that looks like something's growing out of someone's head or if it ends up in a curious position in doing the scene, I try and save that position because I don't like interfering with it. It's like interfering with life. As a parent one wants to interfere the whole time. It's inevitable. You want to say, 'I don't know why you're doing that.' Women with daughters – I've only had sons – but women with daughters say, 'I don't know why you're wearing that, you look much prettier in the other one.' The same with boys, and the same with art.

I remember – it must have been more than fifty years ago – a film called *The Horse's Mouth* with Alec Guinness. He was playing a painter – actually, the story is immaterial. I worked on the second unit, and the production had a painter, John Bratby, who was doing the paintings for the film. Alec Guinness was playing the painter who was supposed to have painted them, and they were lying around in this apartment. After the film had finished shooting, we were doing some pick-up shots, and someone from the art department said, 'Nic, set it up and pan across a painting' – the editor wanted an extra shot of the painting. Bratby did a lot of paintings of his wife, and there was one where she was sitting in a metal bathtub in the garden. It was a semi-rear profile of her and it was all muted colours, sort of off-white colours and grey tints – except at one point: one nipple was just showing. He'd obviously just squirted a scarlet nipple on there – it was startling – and when they put it up on the easel, I thought, 'That's rather extraordinary.' It seemed to me that that point *was* the painting. And the man from the art department came and said, 'That nipple – I don't know what he's done, but it's too scarlet,' and he mixed up some paint. And I said, 'Don't! What are you doing?' But it was too late . . . as he painted over it, the nipple went beige and brown. And standing back from it, he said, 'Oh, that's much better toned down, it was a bit much.' But the painting had completely disappeared – without that one squirt of scarlet, the painting had gone. That one squirt of scarlet was Bratby's truth. You can't reason with truth, you can't reason with it at all.

One time I had a Christmas card with an image by a painter called Norbert Goeneutte: *The Boulevard de Clichy*

The Christmas card

under Snow. He was born in 1854 and died in 1894, and this was painted when he was twenty-one – just a little street scene in Paris. There was something about it that was very filmic: a girl crossing a road and a carriage going away – it was contained in a very small way – it seemed to have a sense of a crowded street and its activity being caught on camera. I found it very real: although it was painted in a very impressionistic way, I felt as if I could step into that place. It said on the card, 'a detail' from the painting by Norbert Goeneutte – a detail – so I thought, 'I must find the painting, I love this detail – it annoys me that there's only a piece of it.' Well, when I found it, it was a painting on a much different scale. The Christmas card was square, and they'd cut off

The painting

a section from each side of the painting. But the whole sense of the original had gone – it was still good, but it was a different painting. It looks more deserted and empty, distant and lonely – it's a lonely Christmas. The other looks like a nice Christmas Day in the Boulevard de Clichy in Paris. It completely changed the atmosphere.

I wouldn't have liked to have been the person who decided to cut off the edges, because it's taking the truth away. But then time goes by and all our truths change, and we owe a debt to film for trying to keep those truths alive as long as possible. As long as possible, the truth in the piece. That applies to pretty well everything, but the art department is an extraordinary place because it gets together all the aspects of it, all the departments of film-making, to try and hold onto their truth. I like working with the production designer and I want them to know what my truth is.

I was talking to François Truffaut once about *Jules et Jim*, where he overrode the costume department. I had said that it was terrific it was so much in its period. And he said, 'I'm so happy you think that. I think so too. The wardrobe people took us to a costume house, and I said, "Let the actors choose what they like," and the artists went and chose the clothes for themselves. And one of the people in the costume department said, "But are they in period?"' And François said, 'I'm not even in my period, I have been wearing this suit for nearly twenty years.' The actors were picking the clothes, generally, according to the atmosphere of the place. So he overrode the costume department. Marit Allen, who was the head of a costume department I used a lot, was marvellous in finding truths like that – allowing what the artists felt was right.

The other day I saw a production of a play by Shakespeare. It was done in a mixture of periods – Victorian clothes and semi-modern dress. And suddenly there was a soliloquy. They were thinking that by putting the character in jeans and a T-shirt it gave a modern thrust to the play. It reminded me of *Clueless* – that American film with Alicia Silverstone. I thought it was brilliant because it was based on a Jane Austen novel, *Emma* – written in 1815. They had the same storyline in *Clueless*, but it was set in modern times. They didn't try and transpose it literally – they had cell phones and things like that. And I kept on thinking about the Shakespeare production. Reinventing the period seems pointless; it doesn't add anything to it, unless you change the whole thing – not just the words, but the attitudes, as they did in *Clueless*.

In some future time – twenty or thirty years from now – the films we're making now will have become period movies, but if we want to remake them, we'll have to transpose the behaviour patterns of that time for the story to be enjoyed. You certainly see it in love stories: with the changes in censorship, people's behaviour, their public behaviour, becomes completely different.

So everyone is part of the movie, but the director is like a jockey. There's the trainer and the owner and the stable lads, but when it finally comes down to it – when it finally comes down to the race – it's the jockey who understands and feels everything that that horse has been put through. At the end of a race, you often hear someone say, 'But you were going to hold back until the very last furlong. I was rather worried when you came round the corner at the edge of the track – you seemed to be going flat out.' And the jockey says, 'She just wanted to go at that point, I could just feel she wanted to go.' That is very, very exciting on a film. From the first shot, the whole unit is making the film. It's wonderful when you sense that they are feeling what you feel about the piece.

It was Orson Welles who said that when you're making a movie, after the first shot everybody else in the crew – from the electricians and the prop man to the hairdresser, everyone, apart from the actors – can make a better movie than you. At least they think they can.

So many movies start the shoot on location – you know, get the exteriors done and then move inside for the interiors. So usually, once the crew's arrived, I like to create a sense of immediacy – the director arrives and gives instructions for what he wants the first shot to be. The crew's standing around, they've got there early and are taking stuff off the trucks; the canteen truck's arrived and the crew are eating sausage rolls, drinking tea or coffee – they're all waiting for you to arrive. And you arrive, and the assistant comes up and says, 'Come on, Nic, everyone's here. We've got it all set up. So what's your first shot?' So I look around and try to find something the whole crew can get involved with immediately. Like if we're in a street: 'See if you can get onto that roof, it would be great to have a long shot. The girl comes out of the building opposite and gets into a taxi – see if you can get us clearance so we can get on that roof. And get the props going. And we'll need it pretty quickly because the sun's coming round and I'd like the sun hitting this side of the road.' 'OK!' – and he's off, doing things, getting permissions. The electricians come: 'Do you want lights for this?' Suddenly the whole thing's under way. The crew is working.

Whether we use the shot eventually . . . it might be the first shot edited out of the film: 'We don't need that establishing shot – she comes out of the building and straight into the taxi.' But that's in the future. In the present, everyone needs to start working immediately, and it gives everyone a sense that you know what you're doing. And it makes it easier for the artist: 'What's the first shot?' 'Oh, you're just coming out of the building. It's simple. Just come out of the building and into the taxi. You can't do that badly; the make-up and hair look great.' So she comes out of the building into the taxi. Everyone's working.

Once everybody's working, just don't forget what Orson Welles said . . . After the first shot, everyone knows better than the director, viz, 'I don't know why he had her come out and then have the taxi turn left, when in the previous shot, etc.' In any case, the first shot is yours. So it doesn't really matter.

The first shot is one of the great mysteries. What is the first shot? You won't really know till the end. That shot may be cut – you just don't know. But the first shot today is from the top of the building.

I was a young camera assistant on *Bhowani Junction*, directed by George Cukor, who was a very well-established director, a totally Hollywood movie-maker. He was rather eccentric and strange, but loved the theatre and was a very unique sort of a guy. It was quite well into his career, and I'll never forget one scene that taught me a lot about attitude within the story: a passing shot where Bill Travers (who was playing an Anglo-Indian) comes rushing to Stewart Granger's colonel – there's been some sort of riot – and he bangs on the colonel's door, and Granger comes out putting on his belt, runs down towards the jeep and they drive off. And Cukor said, 'There's something wrong here, I don't know what it is, Jimmy' – Granger was known as Jimmy, as his real name was James – and Granger asked, what else could he do? And Cukor said, 'I don't think you run. You're a British colonel, and this young man's coming to call you and he has a look of panic about him, and you've got to take it in. Let's have another one where you've already got your belt on and your Sam Brown, and you're walking towards your jeep quickly but not running; he [Travers] is running.'

Granger said, 'All right,' and when he did it the way Cukor suggested, it completely changed the attitude. Granger was right in the character – the calm, walking colonel – and Travers was saying, 'Colonel, we must get there quickly.' Granger: 'Take it easy, son.' I thought it was marvellous – it was just the tiniest little pick-up shot, but Cukor was totally into the scene.

It was marvellous to be young and working with people like Cukor – it was like an apprenticeship, which sadly doesn't happen so much today. It was just a little tip. I remember someone giving me 'just a tip' about many, many things – just a little tip.

The other day someone asked me to look at a little film

– they couldn't think of a title for it. Titles are a very personal thing. I've had many discussions about titles, including
on *Don't Look Now*. I had to have a special meeting with the
people marketing the film because they didn't like the title.
I thought I'd keep my trap shut and not say anything, but I
listened to them for a while, and they went on about how
maybe it should contain something about Venice in the title.
They were just about finishing and they thought they'd won
me over, when I said, 'What is it exactly that you don't like
about *Don't Look Now*? It was Daphne du Maurier's title.'
One of them said, 'Well, it sounds like a B-feature film.' A
B-feature! B-features had gone out of fashion for ages before
that. I said, 'Name me a couple of B-features that it sounds
like.' This brought a typical silence, and I said that what I
liked about *Don't Look Now* as a title was that it was kind of
daring for a movie. First of all, it was definitely du Maurier's
title for the story, and I liked it. One of them had already
said that they didn't because it had a quality about it that
critics would leap on. You know: 'Don't look now – and
don't look any time in the future.' I said, 'That is just what
attracts me about it. If they were to jump in with such an obvious remark, it would be too stupid for words.' In fact, one
critic did! One critic fell into his own trap, into the cesspool
of obviousness! He said, '*Don't Look Now*, and that's enough
said about that.' So I said to the marketing people, 'I want to
keep the title. It's du Maurier's title, and I like it,' and they
fell silent. At that point, the producer, Michael Deeley, said,
'I think Mr Roeg has won his point, gentlemen, don't you?
We'll keep it as *Don't Look Now*.'

Titles are strange. I worked on a movie way back in 1958 with Jack Palance and Anita Ekberg. It was called *The Man Inside*: there were posters along the side of the buses with Anita Ekberg with her hand in front of her mouth as if she was about to scream, and underneath there was the slogan, 'Why did she want *The Man Inside*?' How that got by the censors, God alone knows!

Jack Palance was an extraordinary man. I remember there was a scene where Ekberg had got into Palance's hotel room, and he surprises her there. She doesn't think that he'll be back for some time, but he comes down the corridor and opens the door – that's the tension in it, he's coming down the corridor while she's searching the room – and when he opens the door he catches her as she's about to take something from beside the bed. She looks up and dashes for the door, but he blocks her path. Jack said to the director, 'How do you want me to do this? What does she do?' And the director said, 'Well, Jack, she struggles with you for a minute or two.' And Palance said, 'She struggles with me?' 'Yeah.' 'OK,' and Palance took off. He was a big man – he'd been a heavyweight boxer – and he flew across the room and landed with his arms on either side of Ekberg, and she fell back onto the bed completely under the weight of this man. Then Palance said, 'That's how she'd struggle with me, John.' He then got up and said, 'I'll be back on Monday. Think of a better idea than that. She struggles with me . . .!' Palance muttered as he went off the set. But it was perfect – the action dictated the thought, that was the reality, and it created an extraordinary moment. Action dictating the thought.

Actors

With David Bowie. Me with a cigarette . . . times change!

There comes a time in the affairs of a film called 'the casting'. Apart from all the peripheral advantages of finally casting a film, the moment someone's cast, I feel that part belongs to them. Casting is very, very mysterious – either it happens instantly or the search goes on. There are all kinds of reasons why people are right – it isn't as simple as: 'Oh, they mean something at the box office.' I don't cast for the box office, I cast for the truth. I feel that the part always belongs to someone, and you can sense when it's right.

I have some odd thoughts about casting. I try to work on the script without really thinking who might play a character – I don't like the idea of writing with someone in mind. I've never done it, but I've heard of people thinking, 'It just occurred to me as we were writing the script that it was perfect for "Charley Farnsbarns".' I've never felt that way. I've always tried to avoid thinking about what they look like. I hate it when scripts have 'He was a tall man with a thin moustache' – I can't get it out of my mind then. It precludes things; the story belongs to someone out there – and I like to keep that open. Through the process of working on the script, working on the thoughts, the actual person changes from a tall, dark man to a short, fair man – which I rather like. But there comes a time with the casting when the studio has its own thoughts on the financial side of things. In fact, there's the financial side of casting and the aesthetic side. It's nice when the two come together. But it's very difficult.

There are some very good casting directors. Celestia Fox is exceptional: without putting a stamp on the character, she comes up with a lot. She doesn't limit herself to a type. If, for instance, it says it's a blonde in the script. She thinks inside the piece and suggests artists she can imagine behaving in the manner of the scene rather than the physical description; she knows actors and she knows something about their lives – and that's a very special thing in casting.

Performance is the search for a separate truth. Sometimes it turns out there's a truth in the part that is also a truth in the actor's life – funnily enough more often than not. Once it's cast, when the actor is in the film, that truth can change, and it's very dangerous to try and put them back onto a line of the character which they've somehow abandoned. Then you have to rethink, but that's not a bad idea. The number of times I've heard writers talk about that: 'Well, I'm darned – it didn't start off that way. I didn't think it was such a nasty thing for him to do when he left her, but gradually as I finished the book the ramifications of leaving her were much more than that. Just their love had changed; it affected so many other people – the children . . .' And it's the same with performance. Sometimes it does change the whole film.

I think one should also be very careful about giving the actors scenes to read. Because that's not how it's going to be. I like looking at things they've done. Sometimes they get all uptight – 'Oh no, I don't want you to see that film, I don't like myself in that film.'

I'm not looking at how extraordinary the acting is; I'm trying to see if I can spot a truth in their performance.

I'm also cautious about actors reading the script before they come to a casting session, because I'm not really looking for their opinion about it at that stage. Eventually, yes, but not on first meeting. I have this curious belief that if you can stop interfering with it, people come to the film, come to the story. Curiously enough, this has happened on two or three occasions.

Oddly, on *Don't Look Now*, I remember that when we first began talking about it – I was definitely not thinking of who the actors would be – what was going through my mind was: 'Maybe it would be nice to have an American/British

With Julie Christie and Donald Sutherland

relationship.' I think it was George Bernard Shaw who said that Britain and America are 'two countries separated by a common language' – it's quite amusing, but it's quite true. They understand each other, but in a different way. I had always thought that the two main characters would be a mixed-nationality couple. I thought it would be nice if one of them was French or Italian, but then I decided that I wanted them closer than that. I wanted a pretence of understanding each other – we pretend we understand the Americans, but the Americans are more honest actually: they don't understand the British at all, or they say they don't.

I was just experimenting with that thought, and having worked with Julie Christie on a couple of things as a cameraman – I'd admired her tremendously and her attitude. She began to occupy my mind about being the right person. Apart from being a terrific actress, the truth of her manner was very right for me. Donald Sutherland – I don't know where that thought came from, but I'd known him and admired him, and I thought, 'Even better, an Englishwoman and a Canadian – and a Scots Canadian at that.' They were contacted, but Julie was working for the George McGovern presidential campaign in America and she couldn't do it because the dates were all wrong – and Donald had just started or was in the middle of a film, and he couldn't either. Other people were suggested, and the producers did talk about them because they thought, 'Oh well, that's it, they can't do it, we've got to think of someone else.'

It must have been a sort of stupidity on my part, but I did think, 'It's going to be OK.' And then the McGovern campaign collapsed and Julie became available, and something happened with Donald's film – it went belly-up or something – so he became available, and they both liked it, they understood it. I hardly talked to them at all.

There was a thing that Donald said a little while ago on a closed-circuit talk at an Academy presentation: he said that he'd started to talk to me on the telephone about it, what he felt about it, and I don't remember the incident, but apparently he said: 'I was on the phone to Nic and I started talking to him about it, and I'd been talking for a few minutes and he hadn't said anything but I'd heard a dog barking in the background, and I said, "Nic? Are you still there?"' And apparently I said, 'Yes, Donald. I've got to feed the dog now. Do you want to do it or not?' And he said, 'Yeah, I do want to do it' – and that was the casting session!

Kelly Riley in *Puffball*

On *Puffball*, we were casting in Ireland for the part of the fifteen-year-old girl. We had seen a lot of young people, and I was finishing up a long casting session at one of the schools when the assistant director came up to me and said, 'Nic, there's another girl, she's not on the list, but she's turned up and she's been waiting for a couple of hours. Can you see her?' I said, 'Sure.' And there was something unique about the young girl, Leona Igoe. She had a certain bearing and attitude – I hadn't thought of the character in that way. And I turned to the producer and said, 'She's extraordinary – and to think we might have missed her.' Someone didn't think she'd be right for the part, but in fact there was no doubt in my mind that she was Audrey.

It set the tone for the rest of the casting – everyone I cast, I cast instantly. Kelly Reilly arrived. I'd seen about half a dozen other people, I guess, but as she came in, it was instantaneous. She said, 'I really love it and I want to be this person.' And I said, 'Yes, I'd like you to be that person too.' And she said, 'Good. Is that it?' And I said, 'We'll be in touch – you've got it, you're doing it.' And she left. It was the strangest thing – it was very much the temper of the piece.

With *Insignificance*, practically everyone came to the film. I can't remember a casting session. I remember that after we finished shooting the film, Tony Curtis – who played the senator – came to me in a stunned state and said, 'Is that it? How was I?' And I said, 'You were marvellous, Tony.' Somehow, while we were shooting it, he had moved into that middle-aged part of his life. He had become the senator.

I hate it when people talk about Tony Curtis and say, 'His

Theresa Russell and Michael Emil in *Insignificance*

Tony Curtis in *Insignificance*

real name is Bernie Schwartz.' That was just the name that he was given, or inherited, to identify him at birth. It's not the person he lived his life with and became. When he came out of the navy (he served in submarines in the Pacific during the Second World War) he was just twenty. An atom bomb had dropped on a distant town and suddenly the war was over and he was back in New York, out of work. Any skills he had learned in the services were of no use to him.

Like so many young people, even today, he needed time – 'a gap year' – to figure out the gigantic changes that were taking place in the world. He lived in New York and mixed with a very great cross-section of people: some good and many a bit gang-orientated. By chance, a couple of young men who had also served in the forces had applied, under the G.I. Bill of Rights, for grants to either go to university or learn some other skills. Tony had always been interested in the arts, although he had no experience in any. He put in for a drama course, and with that he fell into life ... as most of us do.

It was at a time when the studios had talent scouts looking for new people from various walks of life and style, both socially and physically. Tony had only been on the drama course for about a year when a talent scout showed up. It didn't take much time before she realised that Bernie Schwartz had great potential, in looks, wit and charm. She recommended him.

The studio she was working for sent for him, and a new birth began. He was given camera tests and groomed in what the studios thought was best for him. One of the major decisions was to change his name, which was quite usual in those days. And young Bernie Schwartz became young Tony Curtis. The studios approved and Tony Curtis was born again at twenty-two.

When I first met him, he'd made over one hundred movies; today that would be impossible for an actor. When we met, it was obvious that the part of the senator in *Insignificance* was perfect for him.

His range of performance was quite unique and he was able to bring a truth to every character he played, and at the same time he never stopped being Tony Curtis. Perhaps that was because he had started life afresh and was able to bring that natural ability to inhabit the parts without trying to over-intellectualise them. Tony was a joy to work with. He had a curious innocence that was both very young and wise at the same time. I think the big studios shaped and formed the artists that they put under contract. They were star makers, and Tony began at the height of that era.

One really quite small incident on *Insignificance* will always stay with me. We were about halfway through the shoot, and during one lunch break I had wandered onto the stage to have a look at the set we would be working on in the afternoon, when I heard someone laughing on the adjoining set, which was the senator's bedroom. It was, of course, Tony. He was half sitting on the bed, reading a magazine. I said, 'What are you laughing about, Tony?' He said, 'Oh, Nic, come here. Take a look at this.' The props people had dressed the set with period things from the time in America when *Insignificance* was set. Among them was the movie magazine that Tony was reading and laughing at, as though it had just come out. He flipped a couple of pages and said, 'Look at this!' It was a full-page glamour shot of a beautiful model. He paused for a few seconds and smiled to himself, then turned to me and, pointing at the picture, said, 'Nic, she is so great.' I saw he was not of this time, but then of course neither was the girl in the picture. She would have been a nice little old lady.

Our memory and the movies keep movie stars alive for us, and Tony Curtis is still a star. Bernie Schwartz died many years ago.

Kirk Douglas and Lauren Bacall were in a film titled *Young Man with a Horn*. It's always fascinated me that, in reality, their names were Issur Demsky and Betty Perske. I don't know why that stuck with me, but as with Bernie Schwartz, there was a lot of name-changing in those days. In the end, it made them who they were. They became their names – much more than their real names – and they'll be remembered as such, with these names, for all time.

I must just add, there is a great little poem by Derwent May called 'A Child in the Eighties'. I think it says it all . . . or nearly all. 'There's still something missing,' as Einstein might have said.

> 'Daddy, how old is Groucho Marx?'
> 'Sorry, dear boy, he's dead.'
> 'Gosh! And Chico? Oh yes, and Harpo?'
> 'Dead. All of them dead.'

'Daddy, is Lassie very old?'
'Dogs die young, you know.'
'Will Hay's good. Is he dead too?'
'Thirty years ago.'

'Daddy, if Elvis comes this way
Can we go and hear him?'
'Elvis stays in Memphis now,
Blue carnations near him.'
'Sossidge is on again tonight.'
'That was Joyce Grenfell, eh?'
'Was? Oh, Daddy, did she die?'
'Just the other day.'

This is immortality,
Never dreamed of yet:
Life because a child sits by
A television set.
'Gary Cooper's good on horses.'
'That was his last ride.'
'Disney must be very rich.'
'Was, until he died.'

But the child who is sitting there
Starts to love each day
People who at natural breaks
Death will take away.
'John Wayne – Bogey – Errol Flynn –
Are they full of lead?'
'Darling, it wasn't quite like that –
But all of them *are* dead.'

Someone recently asked me how I came to cast David Bowie in *The Man Who Fell to Earth*. I'd been thinking of a couple of people for the film: one was an American non-actor – he was a doctor, as well as being a writer and director, but his main occupation in life was medicine. I'd met him at a dinner party. He was obviously an intelligent man, but his intellectual breadth was quite startling, and he was also physically unusually satisfying to look at. He was also six foot eight – so he was startling. Everything about him was right, but it was totally as if somewhere in another world they'd made a person who looked human – like a male human being but they'd got the measurements just a little bit out. I thought that it would be rather interesting if he stood out too much. Then for some reason he felt he couldn't do it . . . but I was really caught . . . he had done something to the whole atmosphere of the film in my head.

With David Bowie on location for *The Man Who Fell to Earth*

And then I was watching telly one day and I saw David Bowie in a thing that Alan Yentob had produced for the BBC called *Cracked Actor*. It was a sort of documentary look at Bowie's life and lifestyle. He had the same sort of qualities, in a curious way, as the doctor. He was unique, he was different in his manner and his behaviour. I started obsessing about that, but there was some doubt about him. People liked him, obviously, but he wasn't an actor, he was a performer – but he was extraordinary.

I went to New York, and we had an arrangement to meet. I think it was something like six thirty in the evening – he was staying in Greenwich Village – and I thought I'd go for a drink with him. And I got there at about twenty past six and they said, 'Oh, he's not back yet, but come in. He's in a recording session and it has gone over a bit, but he'll be back shortly.' I went in. There was a secretary and a PA – we sat and had a coffee and a drink and waited and chatted, watched a bit of television, talked – and time went on and it was about nine o'clock and they were checking with him – 'Please hang on, please stay – at most, he'll be only another hour.' When he finally showed up, it was really late. It was the summer and it had got dark and I think the PA and the other people had drifted off, so I sat there reading a book and it must have been nearly eleven o'clock when they said, 'He's on his way back now.' And he arrived and came bursting in. 'I'm sorry, it just went over – you know what it's like.' Obviously I said, 'Don't worry about it,' but I was a bit pissed off. And he said, 'I really want to do it – is that what you wanted to hear?' and I said, 'Yes,' and he said, 'OK, get in touch – when do you need me?' I said, 'Well, can my people get onto your people tomorrow?' And he said, 'Yeah, any time. I want to bring some people with me. Will your people arrange that?' I said, 'Yes.' 'Terrific, then I'll see you there. Where is it going to be?' I said, 'Albuquerque – we're meeting in New Mexico.' He said, 'Terrific, I'll see you there then.'

It was the most curious conversation.

I got a cab and went back to the hotel, and they said, 'How did it go?' 'It was about three and a half minutes – but it went very well, he's doing it.' I didn't know whether to say I cast him or he's cast me. It was the most bizarre casting, but it was wonderful.

After the first day of shooting, or maybe the second day, one of the executives said – we'd been doing some little pieces, I like beginning slowly for my sake, as well as for the artists'; I don't like getting into a big scene right at the beginning, I just like to see how they look and move, things like that – one of the executives said, 'We're a little worried about his acting – it's a very complex part and we're worried about his acting.' I said, 'What do you mean?' He said, 'Do you think his performance will be able to carry the film?' I said, 'Yes. Frankly, more than anyone else in the film. Why do you ask?' He said, 'I'm just concerned about his acting.' 'Well, how does an alien act? He's pretending to be human.' I thought what he was doing was perfect.

I really came to believe that Bowie was a man who had come to Earth from another galaxy. His actual social behaviour was extraordinary. He brought with him a trailer full of books and things; he hardly mixed with anyone at all. He seemed to be alone, which is what Newton is in the film – isolated and alone. I can't imagine now anyone else in the part. David Bowie is Thomas Newton.

Besides Bowie, I've also worked with Mick Jagger and Art Garfunkel. Performers. There's a very fine line between actor and performer. Performers have to have an extraordin-

Mick Jagger

ary gift of projection or personality. You can learn certain things like voice projection or to always look at someone and then vary it – but there's something odd about the art of performance. In the Hollywood Bowl, there were something like 60,000 people for Mick Jagger. How many straight actors have had 60,000 people turn up for a single performance? Mick gives a performance unlike anyone else. It's an extraordinary piece of acting art.

Another extraordinary example of acting art is in *The Illusionist*, the animated film by Sylvain Chomet. It's a French film set in Scotland, based on an original screenplay by Jacques Tati. I can only think about it, write about it or describe it after stating my unequivocal feeling that it is a 'work of art'. Of course, every detail of the film – the costume design, the props, the dialogue (which is an un-understandable caricature of French or Scots) – can be liked or disliked. You can be bored with it, walk out of it, make rational and possibly understandable negative criticism of it, but none of that would make any difference or take anything away from it being a 'work of art'. It was beautiful and real in such a way that it belonged completely to itself and would be impossible to make again in another format – either on the page or in a 'live' movie. And believe it or not, this is because of the beautiful performances. This is something I have never seen before: the animated actors were wonderful. I have never seen an animated film with such subtlety in the acting that you read the thoughts and silent hopes and dreams of the characters even when they are idly on the screen on their own.

I want to include my feelings about this movie in talking about editing because, although everyone involved should be mentioned, finally the directing/editing are the two things that make it so completely groundbreaking. I can't think of a better title for the film because Chomet and his editors are the illusionists. It would be wonderful – something perhaps linked to the future – if at least one of the illustrated actors were nominated for an Oscar!

The other day I was asked a rather embarrassing question: who did I think was the best actor or actress I'd ever worked with? It's very difficult to talk of 'best' because they're all the best for the particular movie they're in. Acting is a very curious, difficult thing. I've said before I think people come to a film.

Casting is an odd, imbalanced word because it doesn't embrace the fact that I think there's a certain amount of destiny about people that one must be aware of – people are destined for that part. However, I do think that there's a tremendous difference between male and female actors, apart from the obvious ones. By that I mean that women are certainly prepared to take a much broader look at parts than men. Men are very cautious, much more cautious about their 'image' than women – there's masculine fears of being thought weak or emasculated – they're very careful about those parts. Women are much more daring. A handsome man, when he becomes a star, doesn't really like to change his image or act outside the image that's been created – these are general rules – but I find that women are quite excited by changing their image, maybe because they act much more in life. They're much more natural actors, they hide emotions more easily. Men sort of flare up, but women are much more cautious with their emotions, much more thoughtful; they look at parts differently. They don't look at it on the surface, they look at it in much more depth.

Often a woman who's known for her beauty is not averse to playing against that, and because she is prepared to change her image, it actually makes her a greater actress. Men don't like doing that. There was an incident which happened to me some time ago – a part in a script that I really thought would be quite interesting for a man who was known for his rather seductive handsomeness. He read it and said, 'I just can't do this, Nic, I just don't want to do that person.' He didn't want to play a coward – his image of himself was something else. Of course, there are men that do: I think Gene Hackman is a great actor – he's wonderful and his range is very big – but that's why I say it's a general rule.

Actually, it's quite amusing when a woman is cast in a part that goes against how she is imagined. The people who are more frightened than anything are the producers and the studio – until, of course, she proves that it works.

As far as women are concerned, one actor who comes immediately to mind is Charlize Theron, who in *Monster* totally changed her physical look, as well as her personality and voice. After *Monster*, I saw her in something else, and she'd gone back to being beautiful again. It was a startling range: physically she'd changed – her expression, her whole look. I can't think of an equivalent performance from a man. I suppose the only thing that the male actor wouldn't mind doing is something like *Jekyll and Hyde*, where the whole face turns into that of a horrible person – bushy eyebrows and big front teeth – and then at the end, when he's shot, the monstrous face goes away and it's this lovely man again. I don't know why it is – you'd think it would be the other way round, but I've always found that women are much more adventurous. Maybe it's because that much more of their reality is coming out, rather than the fiction of make-up and beauty and hairstyles and fashion.

I respect the art form of acting. I like the fact that we've seen performances change over generations, over years. One of the great artists who changed the whole idea of screen acting was Marlon Brando. When his first film, *The Men*, came out, people said, 'What kind of acting is that? He can't act!'

I wish I'd worked with Brando. He crashed through the whole acting system of Hollywood. He was a unique person, beautiful and more than handsome – rather like some godlike person. I was working on a script of a Friedrich Dürrenmatt book – written with Paul Mayersberg – with a terrifically nice producer, a man called Ray Wagner. He was the producer of *Petulia* – we became friendly on that film – and he loved the idea of this Dürrenmatt book, *The Judge and His Hangman*. Curiously enough, it would be rather apposite today – it's about finance, with a wonderful main character. And somehow it came up in conversation: 'You know who would absolutely love this thing is Brando,' and as we batted it around and talked about it, we began to see no one in the part but Brando. And everybody said, 'Be careful how you approach him, he's crazy – if he feels that you're just doing it to get the film financed . . . He only does things he absolutely wants to do and you never know how to read him.' And Ray was quite friendly with somebody who was vice head of a studio. He'd been Brando's first agent; Brando had engaged him when he was sent for by Hollywood. He flew from New York, and the first person who met him was this very junior agent, and Brando took him on and made him the only person that he'd talk to. So it confounded all the senior executives – suddenly this junior executive was the most important person in the studio because he was the only person that could talk to Brando.

Anyway, Ray said, 'Leave it to me, I know how to go about this, how we can approach him and make it on a much more personal level. We don't want to send him a script, we'll do it differently – we'll call him from your house. We'll say, "I'd love you to read the script," and his people will tell him about you.' So Ray came to England, and the time of the phone call had been set up – we were waiting around for California time. I think Ray came two or three times to the flat and the call was cancelled – and the second or third time they said, 'He's definitely going to be there by seven o'clock your time.' It all built to this peak, it had been perfectly ar-ranged – 'Nobody must use the phone, we must wait for his call.' But somehow things didn't work out exactly the way we expected.

In those days, it was very different from today. You had to book a call and they would put it through. And we were waiting – 7 o'clock came and everyone was prepared. I'd made a lot of notes on how to talk about the screenplay and why I loved it and the book so much. And Ray said, 'When the phone goes, I'll answer it first and then put you on. I'll just chat to him for a little while.'

About five or ten minutes later the phone went – brr-brr, brr-brr. 'This must be it.' Ray picked up the phone and said, 'Hello!' 'Who's this?' and Ray said, 'No, no, no – there must be some mistake! No. Absolutely not. Please, please. No, I . . . There is some . . . I would love to . . .' And it was over.

I said, 'What the hell's happened?'

He said, 'It was Marlon, and I said, "Hello, it's great to talk to you," and Marlon just said, "I don't believe this – you have the goddamned gall to put in a collect call to *me*. And then try and sell me an idea on a collect call. I don't know who the fuck you are! I thought it was an emergency."'

And Ray said, 'I don't believe it, the operator had screwed up and said, "There's a collect call coming, can you accept it from Mr Ray Wagner?"'

The whole project collapsed in about two and a half minutes, with Ray getting a complete bollocking from Marlon Brando. Nobody ever met him again. It was unbelievable – but there it is: the best-laid plans of mice and men.

The story about Ray Wagner reminds me of one about the movie of *Caesar and Cleopatra*, which was based on George Bernard Shaw's play. Shaw lived somewhere in the country, and the producer, Gabriel Pascal, arranged to go down to his country house and talk about what he wanted to do with it. Apparently, Shaw was very interested in all the financial arrangements. Pascal took a train down and then a taxi from the station. He arrived at the house, and Shaw greeted him and they went through things. Shaw said, 'I don't want to talk about maybes and perhaps's. I want to talk about something that's being done, not "perhaps".' But Pascal said he was certain that the money would be there. And as he was leaving he said to Shaw, 'By the way, have you got five pounds for the taxi?' The taxi that had been waiting! And Shaw was so stunned – after having discussed all the financial arrangements – that that was the thing that swayed him: the extraordinary producer-like gall of it.

So you never know . . .

Producers

A nice stripped-down movie camera on a strong tripod with a geared
head for some 'wild' shooting on *The Sundowners* directed by Fred
Zinnemann in Australia, 1959/60

Producers are very different. Personally, I like them – I love tussling with them, especially those who love film. They're not like the accountants, they're not like the distributors; they want it to be a success. It's another creative job – it's rather like an impresario who loves the work, loves the thoughts behind the film. They're very rare now, great independent producers like that.

There's a funny story about Ray Wagner – very much a producer's story. Ray became vice president – I think it was at United Artists or MGM. The studios often did that – get in a working producer and make them a vice president in charge of two or three productions. So Ray took up this job, and of course immediately someone is appointed to something like that they are inundated – everybody gets in touch with thoughts and ideas.

One day someone Ray knew, but only vaguely, got in touch with him and said, 'Ray, can we have a meeting? We'll just have a chat about things.' And Ray said, 'Look, I'm so busy. Have you got a script?' And the guy said, 'No, but I've got something in mind. It's not a script yet.' 'OK, give me a call next week.'

The following week the guy phoned, and Ray's secretary

said, 'Mr So-and-So is on the phone, can you have a word with him?' And Ray said, 'Oh all right, put him through. Look,' Ray said, 'I'm so busy, why don't we meet for a drink sometime?' And he said, 'No, this won't take long.' So Ray said, 'OK, make it tomorrow at three minutes to one. I've got meetings in the morning at twelve and I've got a lunch at one, so I'm saying seriously three minutes.' The guy said, 'Can you make it five?' Ray said, 'No, no, we're not going to argue. You said you could give it to me very quickly – just the general, overall thought. You work on it – three minutes.'

The next day Ray's twelve o'clock meeting had finished. This guy had arrived and was in the outer office waiting, and Ray's PA said, 'So-and-So is here. He's here early, he didn't want to be late for you.' Ray said, 'OK, we've got ten minutes, might as well. Ask him to come in now.'

He came in, and Ray said, 'I can give you five minutes. I know it's ten to one and we've got a bit more time, but I don't want to get into a long conversation about this.'

The guy said, 'I've worked on the thought of it and I've tried to whittle it down, so in three minutes I can tell you exactly. I think you'll get the picture.'

Ray said, 'What is it?'

The guy said, 'Senior citizens bullied in their suburb by a group of young people. Senior citizens learn karate.' He said he saw the whole thing – a comedy-cum-drama, it could go any way.

Ray wanted to do the deal right away. He said, 'Have you

been anywhere else with this?' And the guy said, 'No, I was waiting for you.'

Ray said he felt like putting off his lunch. He said, 'We'll meet tomorrow or we can meet later on this afternoon and we'll work something out.' And that was virtually that. It was just about the time when people were starting to learn karate and judo – it was perfect as a pitch. There was no need for anything else. They did a deal where the studio developed the script. I don't know what happened finally, I think they took it somewhere else – but he got the movie made.

But that sort of quality, you don't find it so much now. That kind of quality of producer was closer to how the studios began. Then, they really wanted stories. Now there's the sense that finance doesn't really want anything; it's all judged differently. The marketing department says whether it's good or bad – there's no single producer/artist or entrepreneur. The people who run studios or the independent production companies – very few of them have that quality, that real old producer quality. Obviously, they haven't gone completely but they're getting rare – they're very rare. Jeremy Thomas is one. He loves movies. He started in the cutting room – there's a lot to be said about producers who gradually come up that way.

I saw a change happening some time ago, a change in the status of the producer, the independent producer, because they didn't rush to the critics so much at one time. Of course, they always wanted to keep on the side of the critics, but they weren't cowed by them, they weren't fearful. Producers like Sam Spiegel – Spiegel loved David Lean's work.

They fell out and talked about things, but Spiegel just liked the work – his comments weren't from some curious bland desire to be popular or anything, his comments were to do with the progress David's movie was making.

I remember a time when I was working on *Lawrence of Arabia*. Spiegel flew out to Morocco to talk to David. We'd been in Spain, where I was doing second-unit things, and then we went to Morocco. David wanted to go back to Spain to do some pick-up shots, and Spiegel was catering for everything he wanted – as much as he could. So Spiegel flew in and called a meeting. We were in the town of Ouarzazate, and he called everybody in to say how much he'd loved the work that was being done and to congratulate all the various departments and their faith in David's movie. David didn't attend that meeting. I remember Spiegel sitting on a little kitchen chair in this courtyard of the hotel and all the crew were there – about a hundred and fifty people – asking him questions: 'When are we going to finish, Mr Spiegel?' 'Soon, I hope,' he said. Then the next day, we were in the desert and I was sitting near David, and Spiegel's plane flew overhead three times in circles and dipped its wings to say goodbye and he flew off. And David said, 'That bugger! After that meeting last night he came and he gave me a line: "I love the work, but I think you're getting nervous, David. We don't need to cover this again." He seduced me into agreeing with him, now he's flown off. He's got a private airplane and he's flown off to see his girlfriend. I fell straight into his trap.' And I thought that was the strangest thing because I'd spoken to Spiegel once on another occasion, and he'd said, 'You know, Nic, I love David's work, I think it's tremendous.' They had an interchangeable attitude with each other of like and dislike. There were very few people who could do that with David Lean – once you didn't agree with him, the shutters came down. It was very difficult to seduce him to a thought of yours – the films were certainly nobody else's but Lean's.

Lean didn't take kindly to any sort of structural or production suggestions. On *Lawrence of Arabia*, the main second unit was run by André de Toth, who was a director who'd done a lot of action films. André was Hungarian, a rather interesting man who'd been married at one time to Veronica Lake, who was a glamorous Hollywood star of the 1940s known for a peekaboo hairstyle – her hair hung over one eye. He was a rather dashing chap himself, mysterious, with a beautiful name. I said to him once, 'It's a marvellous name, André de Toth – did you change your name?' He said, 'No, the family changed the name before we went to America – a long, long time before.' I said, 'Really?' – thinking I was rather a smart-arse. 'Yes,' he said, 'in 1340!'

He had a patch over one eye, which he never really spoke about. I asked him once how he lost the eye, and he said, 'Let's just say that I often visit the grave of the man who did this to me.' It was odd having only one eye because he made one of the first 3D movies, *House of Wax*. Obviously, because he could see out of only one eye, he could never have seen it in three dimensions.

He was brought in to do some battle scenes, and I was photographing them – we did the train crash. He loved

Lawrence of Arabia: the train exploding

David's work and was rather flattered that David Lean had approved of him – and I thought he was rather good – but I'll never forget the day when he came to a sort of confrontation with David because he was full of suggestions about how to shoot the battles. One day he said to me, 'I had this thought last night, Nic. I've done it before, and it's quite an interesting effect.' This was long before CGI; opticals were very expensive, so it was better to do it in the camera. In those days mobile phones weren't in use; it was done with flags – an assistant was behind a sand dune with a flag, waving it. André said, 'I've had this thought about a whole row of glass mirrors, but come with me, I'll describe it to David.'

I went with him, and he said to David, 'May I describe something to you? I'd like to put it into action and get the production to start working on it.' David smoked rather elegant long cigarettes. He said, 'Well, what is it, André? What is it?' He said, 'I would like to get a long wall of mirrors, and the Turkish army are coming towards it and we're photographing them as they're rushing towards us, and hanging behind the wall of mirrors we have bags of blood – big bags of artificial blood – and when the Turkish army are charging towards us, we machine-gun the mirrors – papapapapap-chuh-boom. There's blood everywhere and we have four or five cameras shooting the mirror and the shards of glass and the mirror as we destroy the Turkish army.'

David was smoking languidly: 'That's disgusting, André. Anyway, we'll talk about it later.' And David dismissed him! I thought, 'This is a marvellous idea' – but we never got to do it.

André quit then, so I kind of took over. I last saw him walking around in the desert, and I said to him, 'Have you said goodbye to David?' And he said, 'No, he can go shit in his hat!' And I thought, 'That's not a bad expression either!' And so we said goodbye.

Actually, I heard from him a few years ago. He was retired and I was in Los Angeles, and we suggested meeting. He was certainly a marvellous character. His attitude to film was extraordinary. He's been very underappreciated. He loved film and the ability of the image to tell a story. I thought the shot would have been pretty good because you could use real guns firing at the glass with these blood bags. It never happened. Maybe in the future.

Years later, when I was photographing *Doctor Zhivago*, I got fired. And that story sort of links with André de Toth. On *Zhivago* we were setting up to do the charge of the Cossacks and I'd virtually lit it on paper in the afternoon, not going through the regular process of getting the crew in and then doing it and wasting a lot of time. I thought I could do it on paper, with the chief electrician. We'd measure the power of the lights and what effect they would have – we wanted fifty-foot candles. David arrived and we were lining up the shot, and he said, 'How long will this be? Do you think we should call the artists?' Usually in those days the thing took a whole evening to set up and then we'd shoot it the next day with everybody – just a walk-through rehearsal and laying the cables and things.

And I said to David, 'We can shoot this tonight. I think we can get the first shot before midnight and take an early supper break, and after that we ought to be able to shoot it.' He said, 'What about . . .?' I said, 'I've done it already on paper.' We'd put up the lights as it got dark – they needed some adjustments, obviously – but the main thought, the main focus behind the thought had been done before it got dark. David was a bit concerned. I couldn't think why, and then it became clear later.

We were doing another shot that he'd thought through – only in a vague way. He'd been an editor, and he'd thought it through in terms of the cutting, but he didn't work on the floor as someone who understood the whole. He wasn't so aware of the technical advance of film. He liked to keep it to how he knew it. We'd done a scene on a sleigh with Julie Christie and Rod Steiger with moving lamps and things – we were on a crane – and he said, after I'd made some comment about something, 'You think I'm old-fashioned, don't you, Nic?' Of course, I didn't, but sometimes someone says something and there's no going back on it, no explaining.

We became friends again towards the end of his life, it was OK, but there's a time for coming and a time for going, as there is in all things. And we'd had our time.

The thing I loved about Lean's work, the aspect of him that I thought was terrific – he loved a small story in a huge landscape, and that's an unusual thing because we often fall into the trap of stuffing a huge landscape full of bits and pieces. Everyone loved that famous film of his, *Brief Encounter*, with Celia Johnson and Trevor Howard – that was a big story inside a tiny landscape. It fitted very well: the big story of betrayal in a very middle-class world, dealing with decency and behaviour inside the tiniest landscape of a railway-station buffet bar. But he knew exactly how to expand the story. Talking to him one evening, he said some journalist had been saying how wonderful the film was, and David said to me, 'I can't get rid of it, I can't get rid of it, everybody continually talks about *that* film.' But by then he was on *Lawrence* and he liked moving into this big landscape with the story coming into very sharp focus in that big landscape – a very different attitude, a very thoughtful one. When you think of some contemporary films, they get their impact by building up the special effects – but you don't need it, just isolated moments.

Then there was the scene with Rod Steiger and Julie Christie on a sleigh driving through Moscow at night, and they expected that it was going to take a long time to set up – tracking shots and reverses with lighting on Julie. I said, 'I think we could do this very, very quickly. We could do this with some running shots beside the sleigh – off a car or off tracks. We could get some outboards and I could be on it with a couple of pups' – very small lamps – 'and have the set lit. I could turn the lamps round as we were driving through – swing them round and back the other way – and, as it's running through, cut to when Rod Steiger puts his hand on Julie's leg and cut to her face, and we'd just do it two or three times [swing the lamps], or three or four times with just one angle. Then on another angle and then three or four times the other way to express the confusion of thought – it's gone dark, now it's light, now his hand's on her leg, now he's smiling – that attitude could be done very quickly in the camera. It would be the image taking over the acting.' And David said, 'Have we set it up?' And I said, 'Yes' – and that's when it was over.

Then our relationship started to collapse – very swiftly, within days. I sensed that things weren't going well between David and me. We were OK as far as just talking, but as for my satisfying his needs – we drifted apart. What was weird was that the head of the studio, Robert O'Brien, arrived the night we were shooting the sleigh scene, so he saw the rushes two days later. I got a message from him saying that he wanted to see me, and he said, 'You know, Nic, usually an Oscar is won by having two extraordinary shots on a movie – memorable images – and you've already got three, including those shots of Julie and Rod in the sleigh.'

Two or three days later I had a call from the production department: 'David would like to get Freddie Young back.' It didn't come as that giant a surprise – it was a big disappointment, but I was moving away into other thoughts about film. But I couldn't tell the story of what had happened; it was 'Nic's been fired from *Doctor Zhivago*,' and that was it – and with a thousand different stories for the reason why. It was very difficult for me – a very difficult position to defend – but life goes on and I was going to move on anyway. I wanted to make my own films, I wanted to be further into my own thoughts on the whole art of movies.

So it was good, as it happened. All things are for the best in this best of all possible worlds. It reminds me of those verses from Housman's *A Shropshire Lad*:

> Into my heart an air that kills
>   From yon far country blows:
> What are those blue remembered hills,
>   What spires, what farms are those?
>
> That is the land of lost content,
>   I see it shining plain,
> The happy highways where I went
>   And cannot come again.

Editing

I think the whole idea of editing film has changed. It changed gradually, then suddenly – obviously, with the coming of sound. The next huge change was when editing became digital. Suddenly, it offered so many different choices. When you edited on film, it was put together in the way it was planned; it was even there in the description of the shots: BCU (Big Close-Up), LS (Long Shot), Dissolve, Fade to Black . . ., etc. These were all written into the script because it was much harder to experiment with the construction of the film; you hardly had more than just the ability to select takes. You couldn't press a button and store a whole version of the scene and then come back to it and make comparisons. Digital changed the whole attitude towards editing. In effect, it changed the whole art of movie storytelling.

The speed of change has been very difficult for the studios and producers to take in. Because digital editing gives you so many opportunities and so many different ways to construct the film, people began thinking at speed. We think much faster when many opportunities are given, so many versions can be thought of in the morning, tried out and come back to and changed again.

When sound came, they were just starting to move the

camera – then suddenly they had to have big machines and big cabins to mute the noise the camera made. So films began to be composed as a series of static shots, until the 'blimp' was invented to silence the camera so they could start moving it again, which, in turn, changed the editing and the grammar of the story. Even in literature the same thing happens. I was working with Colin Wilson some years ago, and I told him I really liked a book he'd written called *The Killer*. He said, 'I'm so glad you like it because I must tell you the strangest thing happened when I started to work on it. I went to the Black Museum at Scotland Yard to look at photographs of various murder scenes. They took out one file where there was a picture of a woman stuffed halfway behind a refrigerator, with her legs and a bit of her face jammed up against the back of it. The refrigerator door hung open and stuff had spilled out in a big pool on the floor.' He said the impression of that image as he opened the file startled him, and he thought, 'I'd love to put on the page the feeling I've just had, taking in the whole shock of it in what would be one glance, as in a movie.' However, writing about it, he said he'd have to describe her face and how her killer had obviously jammed her twisted body behind the fridge with her legs sticking out the other side, 'but at the same time I didn't want to drift on a long description. I wanted somehow to capture on the page the visual shock of the scene.' He said he even thought of trying to duplicate the opening of the police file – in terms of the form the printed book would take – so that the shock of the written description came at the point when the reader had to turn the page. I can't think of a more perfect example of the difference between the two art forms – one visual, the other written – than Colin Wilson's description of his reactions.

I watched *An American in Paris* again recently. It's a musical set in Paris around the end of the Second World War, starring Gene Kelly and Leslie Caron. It's charming and really quite delightful. Although obviously dated, it's very much of its time – or, more likely, when it was made, it was probably thought ahead of its time! Anyway, one thing is certain: there is a seventeen-minute dance sequence at the end that is brilliantly devised, performed, choreographed, photographed, directed and edited. Dance is a very, very difficult art to translate to the screen, and Gene Kelly excelled at it and was awarded a special Oscar for advancing the art of choreography. He laid down some lessons on editing physical action and the linking of scenes with movement that is well worth anyone's time today to look at and wonder.

Funnily enough, I looked the film up to check some of the credits and there was a short critique which ended saying: 'The climactic seventeen-minute ballet on the theme of the French Impressionists looks a little precious and "overstaged"' – whatever that means. Well, on looking at the dictionary's definition of 'precious', it means 'of great price or worth, cherished, highly regarded'. However, it's often used ironically for 'arrant, worthless, affecting and over-refined choiceness'. Well, I'll go with the first meaning. Ironic reinterpretations are nearly always suspect. To be fair, the review also said, 'If you haven't seen it, don't miss it.' And that's what I would say to everyone, certainly to anyone beginning work on a film musical or ballet. The last twenty minutes are a lesson in editing 'the dance'.

Tony Lawson is a brilliant editor, and when I was working with him I made him write down each version. As we cut each scene, he'd write down what we felt because if he had to unpick it so that we could do another version, then we could at least reference it back very quickly. In general that was a very rare thing to do – making notes of each scene – but we couldn't just do various versions without ordering reprints for the next day. Just like any of the opticals that we wanted made for the film, the editor would have to measure out and then send to the lab, and the lab would have to interpret what we wanted to do: let it fade in more slowly; not a three-foot fade, make it a nine-foot very gentle fade and then go to three foot and then 'pop' it to black instantly. 'What do you mean by that, guv'nor? You can't – we'd have to then cut it to black.' But now you can do it on your computer: 'Fade to black – now stop it there – and bring it back.' It's amazing.

The editing rooms themselves have changed. They used to be suites of rooms with joiners and splicers and bins to hang up the film strips of the rushes for the scenes the editor was working on. There are no trainees listing, marking and canning the rolls of film. Gone are all the great machines – the Editolas, Moviolas and Steenbecks – where sound and picture were run and cut separately.

Some time ago, I was leaving for LA and was asked if I'd mind taking the cut soundtrack with me of the film we had just finished. They said they'd deliver it to me in the morning, and I thought, 'Oh God, that's ten one-thousand-foot rolls of film to get through customs, etc. . . . Stop the thought! I must be mad.' Of course, the driver arrived the next morning with a little digital cassette in an envelope; no cans, no customs.

The huge technical advances have freed the creative ability of the editor so much, freed even the screenwriter, whose detail of the shots – i.e. 'Cut to' or 'Pan off', etc. – had to be more strictly held to a lot of the time, just for budget or schedule reasons. 'Script approval' embraced how the film was shot and cut. Since editing has become much more part of the very essence of the film rather than just the delineation and construction of the story, film has begun to get a life of its own.

We think God's work – such as the sunflower – looks the same to everyone, but the painter looks at it in a different way. Just as he is expressing his personal vision, so it should be in all acts of creative expression. In making a movie the ability to experiment with a scene and instantly make comparisons with a different construct makes the editing of a film the final major creative act of the whole work. I can never understand a director not being a part of that process. Until now, commerce and corporate censorship had almost completely controlled the creativity of movie-making, but that is gradually changing and will soon become a thing of the past. There is nothing more dating, whatever the situation, than 'We always do it that way.'

Some time ago in Hollywood there was a writers' strike, which I thought was very strange . . . artists going on strike.

I could understand it from a commercial point of view, but I thought it would only be effective for a very short time, and then only for the established writers, and really only threatening to productions about to begin. In some ways the strike could have been a positive thing, insofar as the work is concerned. It possibly opened the door to alternatives and other ways to go. New, unknown writers struggling to be recognised might have got a break – no one is indispensable in any of the arts. A new way of thinking might even be the very thing that's needed. That's the beauty of the arts. They are constantly moving, constantly changing, and they overlap with each other. This is especially true with the movies, which are such a diverse amalgamation of so many creative works – from the word to the performance, even to the sex, race and nationality of the performer. Often a radical change can be inspiring.

I feel it's wrong – except from a corporate point of view – to plan too much. I've always said, 'That's what makes God laugh, people who make plans,' and it certainly brings on a lot of disagreement if you establish plans and they don't work out, or you change your mind. In movie terms, there's nothing worse than changing your mind. In fact, I believe there's nothing better in terms of movie-making than being open to change, because when you're being definitive, 'You don't see the gold beneath your very feet,' as old Walter Huston said. Of course, it's a very delicate balance, making something before the film has been shot or before the scene's being enacted or come to life – to have made plans, very strict plans about it. Years ago, when I was a young assistant,

I'd watch people consult the script: 'It says here . . . This is the plan,' and I'd say to the camera operator, 'Look behind you, look over there. Why don't they . . .' 'Shhh, Nic, be quiet.' 'But it looks so great – the sun's going down.'

I'm not saying don't prepare anything – you can have a sketch, an outline. But all kinds of things can happen, so be open so that you can seize the moment. It's difficult in life to be certain. The people who walk straight into a brick wall at high speed really believe that everything is going to be exactly how they planned it; they're always surprised. Boing! 'That wall wasn't supposed to be there! It wasn't there yesterday.' And that's what happens with editing. I've had very lucky experiences with terrific editors, but it's a very delicate and strange relationship. In the early days, the editors thought, 'Oh, he's letting me do it.' We'd start getting the scene together and we're making selections, and then gradually I have to get them to understand: 'Yes, we've put it together in that way, but now let's have a look at it another way. Let's examine all the other stuff because I shoot a lot of stuff.'

My mind is drifting the whole time; various things are popping into my head. I would hate to be put in an empty room. I need my books around me and I need to move about, I need to look and think – and, if I get stuck, to go out and walk around – because something always presents itself. I can't think through things without being reminded of other things. I'm not saying it should follow the story. I believe that's what happens in life – things suddenly remind you of something. Is it a coincidence, as I look at my bookshelves, that I see *The Probability of the Impossible, The Challenge of Chance, The Roots of Coincidence*?

From the very first day I got the job as a runner and tea boy at the De Lane Lea dubbing and post-synch cutting rooms, I was hooked by the magic of moving pictures. It's difficult to imagine now, but I had absolutely no knowledge whatsoever of the process of post-production and editing. For me, seeing that cutting room was the same as a young boy today being shown the possibilities of a computer. Probably even more than that – the computer is of its time and is part of life now, and is as familiar and commonplace as the microwave oven or the flush toilet. One must remember there was no TV then, and I couldn't conceive that you could run film, stop it and start it, make it go backwards and forwards while sitting in front of the Editola and just turning the handle. I could even play with the soundtrack and run that separately. It was fantastic . . . and the thoughts and possibilities of that time in the cutting room have stayed with me all my life.

When I was shooting *Walkabout*, there was a scene where the young boy is in a state of shock and sadness as he sees two hunters shoot a buffalo. The boy gazes at the killing of the animal, and with the simple reversing of the animal falling we put it back up again and intercut it with the boy staring. It becomes a beautiful moment in the thoughts of a child. The thrill of what can be done with the retained moving image and linking it to our behaviour in life has never left me. 'If only we could put the clock back' – isn't that what's often said? Well, in film we can.

In *Bad Timing*, the film moves – with thoughts and situations – apparently randomly between present, future and past. Well, that's how I always imagined how people feel about time, how they review their lives: moving between memory, the present moment and their hopes or fears of what's to come. I remember being told by some journalist – I think it was a French one – 'You make it very difficult for someone to understand what you're thinking.' Well, I'm trying to be as honest with my thinking as I can be, but everybody's thoughts are secret, and when we come to the point where we allow ourselves to reply to someone, it's only about a quarter or a fifth of what we have been thinking quickly in our minds. What is that Jungian thing? There are five stages of thought before you answer a question: 'Should I tell him?', 'Is he ready for this?', 'Will he understand?', etc. – all these various stages of thought happen automatically in the mind. Some people tell the truth more with a lie than they do by telling the truth. When we are lying, it tends to be beautifully done in terms of detail: the liar can remember everything, which must, in human terms, be suspicious. Not definitely untrue, but suspicious.

Again in *Bad Timing*, Dr Linden, the psychologist, angrily blurts out in disgust to Milena, his lover, 'My place is beginning to look like your place.' What he is really saying is, 'Why don't you behave as I do?' He feels he is the one who is being controlled. If she tidied up her room, which is in the untidy state of a rather bohemian young woman's home, he would be happy. It would be definite proof that she loved him. However, Milena responds in a rather offhand, jokey

Theresa Russell and Art Garfunkel in *Bad Timing*

and dismissive way: 'Then why don't you go back to your place?' She doesn't think it's such a big deal, but it's the start of the break-up of their relationship.

They have reached the point where joint needs and desires must be served. If one has to sacrifice an attitude of behaviour, that's the first step to being controlled. So often break-ups begin with an offhand comment that reflects the inner character or secret true personality of one of the partners.

It's sad, Alex's love of Milena is doomed from the start – no matter how long it takes. It starts with pretence on his part, a blindness to the beauty and truth of who Milena is. It is also sad because at the very end of the movie he sees all the beauty of her disarray – 'Well, I'm damned.' With the end of any hope of the control he so badly wanted, he sees the charm and beauty of her life, which he can now never share. 'Late have I loved thee' – that's what we all say in the end.

I remember once when I was working on a script with Paul Mayersberg – I think it was *Eureka* – we came to a moment that exploded into an action sequence, and Paul said, 'Oh! This is a "cavalry comes over the hill" scene, Nic. Just let's push on. You're only going to change it, even when you're shooting it.' And he was right. Not only would I have changed it at the shoot, I would also almost certainly have done so when we came to edit it.

When you begin the edit, you are taking the last creative stand. For me, it can nearly always feel like the final and most daring moments of making a movie. Somewhere I either read or heard that wonderful maxim about the creative process: 'First kill all your darlings.' It's difficult to do, but once done, it's usually for the better. It ends all sense of vanity.

Another trigger for emotion that film can express more perfectly than any other form – especially when linked to music – is memory. I loathe the term 'flashback' – it has come to mean a cinematic gimmick and is generally attacked by the critics. But our memory and our thoughts are constantly going backwards and forwards like a clock, tick-tock, tick-tock, tock-tick, tock-tick. Someone says to you, 'Did you have a happy childhood?' and your thoughts go back to how you were as a child. For me the answer would be, 'Yes, I had a happy childhood.' Then if asked, 'What was it like?'

I'd probably have to say, 'If I told you, you'd think I had a terrible childhood.'

I had a very distant father in terms of how he appeared to be, but in fact he wasn't – we just had another form of contact and understanding between us. He'd had a strange and very difficult life. He never spoke about it but somehow, metaphysically, he conveyed that to me. He seemed to be quite distant as far as other dads were concerned – he didn't take me camping or fishing or help me carve something – but as I'm telling you this, I can't explain how differently I think of him. In my memory he still amuses me. I quote him a lot. His odd sayings went very deep into my thoughts, and the things he said I've said and my sons say now. He's still alive in them.

A sense of that kind of memory was done beautifully in the Ingmar Bergman film *Wild Strawberries*. There is a very moving scene when the old man is coming up to the city for an award of some kind, and he stays with his son and daughter-in-law, who are having a problem in their marriage. The son takes the father up to the bedroom with an 'OK, this is your room, Dad' attitude. The father lies down on the bed, just as the son comes back upstairs and says, 'Are you OK? Everything OK? I'll leave this door slightly ajar.' The father nods and turns over to face the camera, just as, in the background, the son and daughter-in-law are whispering and having some sort of a row. The old man is turned away from them and you can see him starting to drift off as he lies looking at the camera, and as the camera moves into his eyes we cut to a boy running. He's dressed in a rather old-fashioned way and we hear him panting – huh, huh, huh – as he runs across the field and up onto an embankment, where there is a canal. He looks across it and sees, sitting on the other side, a young woman with a parasol and a man sitting next to her – obviously his parents – and they look across and wave at him. It still moves me even now, when the boy looks across and smiles at the young couple and knows he's safe and turns and runs away. And then we cut to the old man in bed, smiling as he shuts his eyes. A beautiful moment in the most superb film. That is movie storytelling. How can you possibly do that on the page?

Love Scenes

My thoughts about . . . bits and pieces for a sex scene
(drawn by me, aged seventeen)

Sex and death are the only things that can interest a
serious mind.

William Butler Yeats

Desire. I ponder that a lot. Love and desire don't necessarily
go together. It's very nice if they happen to come together,
but then they part. Sex. Desire. Love. They're all related to
romance and the romantic notion of stories. But Romance
is completely different. Romantic stories very rarely show
anything physical in them. It's a perennial theme, isn't it?
Dante and Beatrice – love from afar. But it's very difficult
to slide romance into reality – not that I'm not a romantic
– but it's very difficult, that bridge from romance to love
to sex – 'Whoops! I'd better keep that out, slip it in somewhere under the table!' I think there's a return right now
to romance. Love scenes have become so acceptable, but the
way the reality of the sex is being filmed, it's become so
blatant that it's becoming closer to pornography. But everyone's view on what is and isn't pornography is different. And
is pornography always a bad thing? So the feeling seems

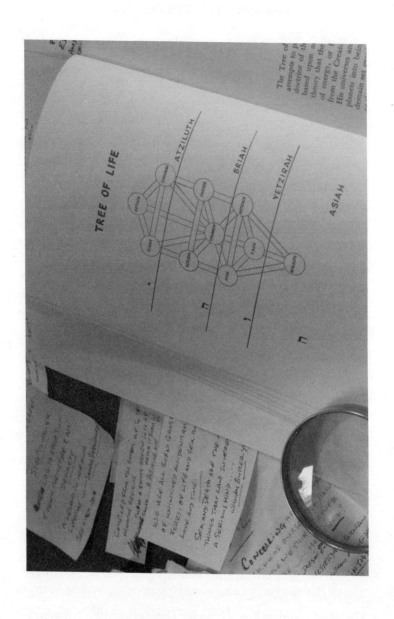

TREE OF LIFE

to be: 'Let's do away with it altogether, let's just have it romantic.'

I worked on a film about Oscar Wilde – Peter Finch was Oscar. There was no love scene; in fact, homosexuality wasn't even spoken about in the film. There was nothing, but today I'm sure they'd have a bedroom scene with Oscar and the young peer. Maybe not today, but yesterday! Today, it would be back to romance. I think *Brokeback Mountain* just had a little moment of kissing, didn't it? And that was deemed to be OK.

Desire is very difficult to portray on screen, and the audience has to believe that someone desires someone. It's so difficult to figure out how to talk to the artists about it. Usually it's very superficial: 'We're going to do the "love scene" now. Darling, get your nightdress on . . . Would it be all right if you wore your boxer shorts? . . .' How do you act that? I watched it when I was a camera assistant: You'd see the actors whispering to each other, then the director says, 'Turn over,' and they'd lie down and kiss and then glide down the body . . . But, to me, it's not real, it's superficial.

Woody Allen had a marvellous line. I think it was in a film with Diane Keaton – I can't remember which one – but it amused me because Keaton and Allen were an unlikely couple. They look across the road, and there's the most handsome man and a beautiful woman walking hand-in-hand, and Diane Keaton says in an incredulous way, 'Who are they?' and Woody says, 'Oh, they're Mr and Mrs Couple.' The ideal couple – but, of course, the ideal couple doesn't exist in reality. I prefer: 'What on earth does she see in him?' or

'What does he see in her?' – that's the reality! It's the biggest thing in life – not only the sex, but the actual living together and how we see each other. You can love someone even though your sexual balance isn't exactly the same. Every part-nership, every marriage goes through waves of ups and downs, and it's lucky if it stays teetering in the balance of: 'Well, I'll sacrifice something in order to hold onto the other.'

We can change the whole attitude towards a character based on the form their desire takes. Mutual desire is fant-astic, but it's very rare. I have desires! Mutual desires, I hope. The real dig of the knife is: 'Not only do I not love you any more, I have no desire for you.' That's hell.

Actually, it happened to a friend of mine – an actor, a dear, dear friend of mine. He fell in love with a very beautiful woman. They were both young, and he was rather socially shy, even though he was an actor. They got married, and after they'd come back from their honeymoon, he said to me, 'Can we go for a drink?' I said, 'Yes. What? – is everything OK?' He said, 'No, we're getting a divorce.' I said, 'What!'

He told me the most extraordinary story: they went off to their honeymoon in great excitement, throwing confetti and streamers, with rattling tin cans at the back of the car, and they were so happy. They went to a hotel in France, and the first night, he said, was marvellous – this was in the days of long engagements; they hadn't been living together, but they had made love. Previous to this relationship, his bride had had a long affair with another friend of mine, Nigel, who was a bit of a curious bloke. So my friend says to me, 'It was extraordinary, Nic. It wasn't the first time we'd made love, but it was the first time in our marriage. I was consummating the marriage. And the next morning we were having break-fast on the terrace, and I put my hand out and squeezed her hand and said, "It was just marvellous, darling. Was it as great for you?" And she said, "Yes it was wonderful."

'"Really?"

'"Yes, it was wonderful. It was just different."

'"What do you mean?"

'"Well, it was wonderful – but I just couldn't *wait* to get into bed with Nigel."

'"What?"

'"But it was nothing, darling – he was an awful person."'

My friend said to me, 'I couldn't believe it . . .' and nearly broke down. His wife was very young – twenty-two or something – and was saying it in all innocence, not realising the effect it would have on her husband. They divorced after waiting some months – they didn't want to create a scan-dal – and he married again, as did she. They tried to remain friends, but it didn't work out.

He and I stayed friends until he died. His story moved me tremendously – I know it's tipped off my thoughts about these things, and in *Puffball* there's a scene where one of the characters can't quite match another character: 'But can't you forget it?'

'No.'

'But I forgive you.'

'It's not a question of forgiving'.

Love can be very painful, it can be a very selfish act. A

friend of mine's daughter was an air hostess. She was in an accident – the plane crash-landed in the Bay of Naples. She was helping people get out, down the chute into the water. There was a man with a child, and he couldn't swim. As he was paddling desperately, he pushed the child away and she drowned. Nature was telling him to save himself.

Love and sex don't have to go together. More often than not, they don't. What isn't often touched on is the reason for sex – procreation. Obviously everyone knows that, but it's ignored in stories. The reason for a love scene is that the characters are physically attracted to one another – but the reason behind this attraction is to procreate. Schopenhauer said that the genius of the genes inside you dictates desire.

When we were doing *Puffball*, they were worried about censorship – you see a penis going into a vagina, sperm unites with an ovum. You see it all the time in nature programmes. It's a crucial part of *Puffball*, it's part of the characters' story – it's about the nature of life. But people talk about it as if it's ugly. But two years later, when the same thing is shown in *Antichrist*, no one's disturbed about it. Nowadays, you almost expect it. In the old days, it was forbidden to have two people in the same bed. Married people had to have separate beds – you certainly couldn't have a man and woman in bed together. A man could sit on a bed, but he had to have his feet on the floor. Censorship is lunacy, but it's always with us. But in life, fortunately, manners change.

I did a love scene that has become very well known – the one in *Don't Look Now*. Originally, it wasn't in the script. We hadn't thought about it before. So we started shooting and gradually, as the film developed, the characters played by Donald Sutherland and Julie Christie seemed to be arguing all the time. Of course, there were reasons for this bickering – the death of the child, stress – but I thought, 'This story needs something, their plight needs a pause, a breath. There needs to be some kind of intimacy between them.'

They're going out to dinner, and I thought it would be nice to see them getting ready. Julie Christie is having a bath and Donald Sutherland is in the bathroom, naked, brushing his teeth. Then she gets out of the bath, dries herself, flops down on the bed and starts looking through a magazine. As Donald enters the bedroom, she refers to something in the magazine – 'Here, look at this' – so he flops down on the bed and casually takes her hand. She touches his back. They kiss, make love, and then they go off to dinner. People said, 'Oh, that's a very sexy scene.' Of course it was sexy; it's be-

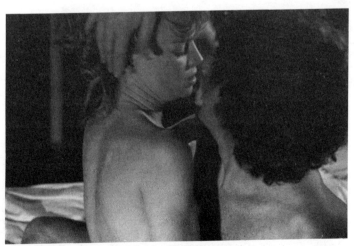

Don't Look Now: the love scene

cause it had truth in it. There was a normality to it. The truthfulness came from the characters, because of who they were. The studio said, 'We can't have that.' The censor put an 'X' certificate on it in America. But there was nothing outrageously explicit about it.

It was only after we had shot the scene, later that day, that I got the sense that maybe it was the first time they'd made love with that degree of giving and romance since the death of their child. That it was the perfect moment for a child to be conceived – which would be some kind of comfort in their grief. A new life, making up for the death of the child. When we were shooting the final scene when Julie is on the funeral barge, I told her to lift the veil from her face. When she asked me why, I said that she knew she was pregnant and that she should have a slight smile on her face.

Don't Look Now: on the funeral barge

Desire is so delicate, so dangerous. So when you approach a 'love scene', actors can tell if it's just gratuitous – you know, 'Clear the set, boys,' and all that rigmarole. I couldn't not do that – and nobody could say I was a prude – though sometimes the reverse happens: the more delicate you are, the more pornographic it becomes, because there's no truth in it, no heart in it, no development of anything. That's why *Don't Look Now* needed the love scene to make their pain more believable.

When *Don't Look Now* was first shown on the BBC, they cut the love scene, but there were so many protests that they put it in the next time they showed it. A few summers ago it was shown on a huge screen outdoors – and no one said a word about the love scene!

There was one occasion on *Bhowani Junction*, directed by George Cukor, when we'd been waiting all morning for the actors – Ava Gardner was in make-up and Stewart Granger was doing something or other. We were all waiting and waiting. We'd already lined up the shots with their doubles – 'How long will they be?' 'Certainly within the hour' – and Cukor said, 'You know, all we really need?' – *Bhowani Junction* is about a love affair between an Anglo-Indian woman who is in the Women's Auxiliary army and a British colonel, and we were back from location in Lahore, back in England, and we'd built this set that looked like part of the railway station. And the whole film is centred around the affair – and Cukor said: 'You know, all we would really need is a big nice comfy mattress and have 'em come on and sit on it and start making love – and then we'd be out of here and it would make the same amount of money!' It sounds like a vulgar thing to say, but that's really the root of everything: 'The only things that can interest a serious mind are sex and death.'

That's it: procreation and death. It comes back to the child asking, 'Why am I here, Mummy?' And it's usually when they go to bed. Well, Mummy and Daddy are stumped. They don't say, 'Well, you're going to be an account executive with a big insurance company.' What they do say is, 'You're here because Mummy and Daddy love you, and don't you worry your head about that, and . . . Shh, I'll leave the door open and if you want anything just call me.' And you leave the child thinking, 'I'm here because Mummy and Daddy love me. What does that mean?'

In *Puffball* there are four love scenes – four physically emotional scenes. They're love scenes and sex scenes and

Puffball: Rita Tushingham, Leona Igoe and Miranda Richardson

man-and-woman scenes. And all four are completely different. They're different ways of making love – and for different reasons.

The characters have certain ages: from a foetus to a girl to a young woman to a middle-aged woman to an old woman – the various stages of womanhood. And their desires or their fears or their hopes are all mixed up in it, so that when there are love scenes – or sex scenes – you know that sex is part of their life. They're people with different qualities and different needs. Although one of the scenes might seem to be rough, it's not a 'rape', it's a different attitude. It's a love scene that takes place, as far as one character is concerned, on the spur of the moment, but the other one has been thinking about it all afternoon – and that's part of the plot of the film.

The film is more character-driven than plot-driven, so I like to think of the love scenes as part of the character development. Without those love scenes, the characters wouldn't have developed in the way they do. They display who the people are and what the reasons are for the way they behave – though their intentions may be quite secret.

Recently I saw a film by Bernard Rose based on Tolstoy's novella *The Kreutzer Sonata*. Danny Huston plays a man who's becoming insanely jealous of his wife for no reason. Jealousy sometimes breeds itself, it dangles things in front of a person's mind so that they start believing that there's something going on which, in reality, is quite innocent. He's reaching that stage of psychosis, while still being charming. There's a scene where he comes home at lunchtime for something, and she's on the phone, and he starts to feel her up and impose his desires on her. She doesn't want to disturb him or upset him, so she's patting him on the head and trying to fend him off while she's talking on the phone, and he's getting more and more angry because she won't put the phone down – and suddenly she's had enough. You see her change – at first, she was rather amused by it, but then she realises: this is getting nuts, this is nothing to do with sex or love or desire or anything at all. It's jealousy. And there's a marvellous moment, I can still see it: she puts the phone down, gets up off the sofa, pushes her skirt down and says, 'What the hell's going on? What's wrong with you?' It's a marvellous moment of confrontation – she could see that his attitude had nothing to do with love; it was all done without a bit of feeling. And at that moment of confrontation, you could feel truth was there, you could sense that the actress knew exactly what she was feeling – she wasn't pretending. It was very good.

I thought it was a really interesting reflection of the secrets in our life. She had no idea that he was so jealous of her. It was probably his own actions that made him suspicious – there's that corny old line that your hatred of something is due to your hatred of yourself.

Audiences tend to identify with the characters they see on the screen, so with love scenes they have a curiously ambivalent attitude towards what these characters are doing. So it's easy for the audience to reject them: 'I don't want to see this.' Because if you're with a character, you're scratching the surface of a more secret side of yourself – and you don't want to give yourself away by saying you're enjoying yourself.

In fact, you're giving yourself away when you say what you don't like. Oscar Wilde said, 'All criticism is a form of autobiography.' When R. D. Laing was asked to view a film I made called *Bad Timing*, he said it had the qualities some works have of alienating the audience. They don't mind seeing it alone, or reading it secretly, but they don't want to be seen enjoying it.

Mirrors

Orson Welles and Rita Hayworth in the mirror scene
from *The Lady from Shanghai*

Mirrors are really fascinating. The mirror is a very strange thing, and yet so simple. There's the Greek myth of Narcissus using the pond as a mirror and losing himself as he stares into it. Mirror shots have always been clouded in a sense of mystery. I really love them – they are the very essence of cinema.

One of the great mirror sequences is, of course, at the end of Orson Welles's *The Lady from Shanghai*. The whole film builds to its height in the hall of mirrors, with gunshots going off and all the characters being splintered into tiny pieces; visually, not only their lives were shattered, but also their hopes, plans and dreams.

Mirrors have such an effect because it's the only time we really have a look at ourselves. With photography, we see ourselves as others see us, but not with that penetrating look – the privacy of ourselves looking into the mirror.

I used a mirror in *The Man Who Fell to Earth*, in the scene when Newton dares to revert to his natural/unnatural state. Mary Lou is outside the locked door of the bathroom, while inside he takes off the covering over his eye, revealing himself. She's desperate to see him and says, 'Tommy, it's OK, Tommy, I don't care . . . What are you doing? I love

Newton in the bathroom

you.' He believes her and reverts to the alien he is – we see him in the mirror. He opens the door and she screams, and instantly he puts it all back on again.

Similarly in *The Witches*, when Anjelica Huston is starting to take off the friendly human image of her face to reveal the grotesque look of the witch. She's surprised by a knock on the door and she puts the human image back on – back to being a normal person. When the person who interrupted her leaves the room, she then exposes herself as who she really is again.

There's a certain truth in mirrors – a sort of surreal truth. They're reflecting things all the time. The mirror is, for me, very much part of film, cinema and the retention of the image.

On *Don't Look Now* in Venice, when Julie Christie goes to the ladies' room, two old women interrupt her there, and the scene is all shot in the room's three mirrors. She's reflected twice, and the women are reflected differently and at different times in different shots – as one leaves, the other comes back into the mirror. I think something so mundane and ordinary as seeing the scene through a mirror somehow sets up a mystery or a revelation of something.

I love mirror shots. I love them because they somehow do something with the character. It isn't part of the narrative and it isn't part of the performance; it's like spying on someone – even spying on themselves.

In *Castaway* Amanda Donohoe plays a young woman who's gone to live with a relative stranger on a deserted island where they've deliberately stranded themselves – she's not really thought about the incidentals they'll need, such as a mirror. It seems so obviously ordinary. But, somehow or somewhere, she's found a broken mirror that she fixes on a tree. There's a short scene where she's looking in it, and the

The Witches: Anjelica Huston removing the friendly face

shattered mirror doesn't connect to make a single face, the little bits of shattered glass reflecting odd bits of an overall image – and it was absolutely right for the movie. It would be rather pretentious to say, 'Oh, that was the reflection of a shattered relationship' – no, it's a visual moment of truth. A moment of truth in a mirror, that's where people examine themselves. A lot is revealed when one is caught looking in the mirror at oneself.

In *Eureka* we were shooting in this wonderful colonial house, and like many of those great houses it had a big mirror in the hallway before the staircase so that people going upstairs or arriving and giving the butler their coats could check themselves out in it. In the last scene Rutger Hauer leaves Theresa Russell. They are having dinner privately together upstairs on the veranda, and he says he'll be back in a minute, gets up to leave and we see him coming into the hall. He goes across the hall and appears to be saying goodbye as he looks at things, then he looks sideways and sees the mirror. He goes right up to it and talks to himself as though saying goodbye to himself – that life, it's now in the past, the past would be held by the mirror. He's virtually saying – in fact, he does say – to his reflection, 'I knew it would be you.' He nods and puts his head against the mirror, then he's gone. Seeing that scene still moves me because we shot it near the end and so much is summed up in it for me, although maybe not for a lot of people – they have their own mirrors. It certainly worked for me – and for Rutger, I think. The part spilled into himself.

Eureka was the story of Jack McCann, a prospector. It

Eureka: Rutger Hauer: 'I knew it would be you.'

was based on Harry Oakes, who was the most extraordinarily successful Canadian prospector who struck gold. We
began the production with great excitement, but then – it
was one of those things – the timing was bad. The whole
political and social and artistic culture was changing, becoming much more materialistic. So when we finished it and
it came out in 1982, it was completely out of tune with the
times and people were confused by it. The film was saying
what the first verse of Robert Service's poem 'The Spell of
the Yukon' says – gold isn't all:

> I wanted the gold, and I sought it,
>   I scrabbled and mucked like a slave.
> Was it famine or scurvy – I fought it;
>   I hurled my youth into a grave.
> I wanted the gold, and I got it –

Came out with a fortune last fall, –
Yet somehow life's not what I thought it,
And somehow the gold isn't all.

In our story, Jack McCann suddenly realises that the gold isn't everything, but when the movie came out the whole idea of ambition and getting on and making money was in full force. And by 1989, *Wall Street* had come out and greed was good! It was at the very, very peak of its time. It hit everybody: 'Greed's good, don't worry about it.' It crumbled afterwards, but by then *Eureka* was long gone.

The very root of all business is making money – and a prospector is such a unique character. It was marvellously summed up by McCann: 'I never made a nickel from another man's sweat' – that was the rule he lived by. I thought it was terrific that he owed nothing to anybody, that it was him that did it all. At the end, McCann's wife says, 'I don't know why

Eureka: Gene Hackman as Jack McCann

they don't like you.' 'It's not me they dislike, it's what I stand for.' It couldn't be more on the nose than that.

Generally speaking, I don't like having any political lectures inside movies – I don't like to take sides – but I like observing the situation, observing the time we're living in, and trying to find some sort of core value. One's always swimming against the tide of thought and hope. Although I've always had hope in a movie.

'Somehow the gold isn't all' – that's a great beginning to a poem. I've always thought it might be better if it was the last thing that we hear in the movie. It seemed the appropriate end to his story. But the last verse is quite wonderful too:

> There's gold, and it's haunting and haunting;
>   It's luring me on as of old;
> Yet it isn't the gold that I'm wanting
>   So much as just finding the gold
> It's the great, big, broad land 'way up yonder,
>   It's the forests where silence has lease;
> It's the beauty that thrills me with wonder,
>   It's the stillness that fills me with peace.

That's good for the ending too because he suddenly realises that it's OK to have lived his life, and he sees the beauty just at the last moment.

It's rather like the story of the man in America who had been a villain all his life: he'd been on the run, been the 'most wanted', he'd been in junior prisons from the time he was fourteen, then he got a life sentence for two murder charges in one state, but he'd done a bunk and got across the border to another state. Then, finally, he was caught and sentenced to be hanged. He was angry at the sentence because the crimes were in another state, and he'd never shown any fear or remorse for anything he'd done.

This was in the Midwest somewhere, and they put up the scaffold just outside the walls of the prison so he could see across the great plain of the state he was in – great plains of wheat fields. He was to be executed at dawn, and he went up to the scaffold and the hangman adjusted the rope around his neck – and they looked at the horizon. The sun was just coming up and they waited until it was fully up. The great golden light across the wheat fields fell on his face and he turned to the hangman and said, 'It *is* a beautiful world,' and they put the hood on his head – bang – finito. But he'd seen it once.

I always thought that story was marvellous because very often you go through life and you don't see the beauty of it all. So there was a lifetime in that gaze, in those few seconds: 'Well, I'm damned – it is a beautiful world.' And that reminded me of Jack McCann at the end: it wasn't just the cold arrogance of, 'I never made a nickel from another man's sweat – it's me – I did it.' He sees the beauty of how he lived his life.

Some time ago I took part in an arts programme on painting for the BBC. The general theme was: 'What paintings are you drawn to?' And I chose the *Rokeby Venus*. It's a painting I like very much in terms of its storytelling. It's very much like a still from a movie; it's very photographic. This beautiful young woman is lying, looking at herself in a mirror – it's from the painter's point of view and the reflec-

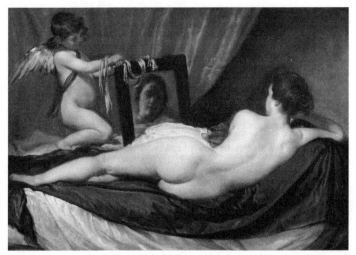

The Rokeby Venus by Velázquez

tion of her face in the mirror is all soft focus. The 'in-focus' section is her bottom and her hips. Now, when we look at something our focus changes all the time, automatically. We take in the 'wide shot', as it's known in the cinema, and everything seems to be in focus; then we look at something in 'close-up' and that particular thing becomes in focus and everything in the background is not – we're switching focus to what we've selected to look at in particular. That is what draws me to the *Rokeby Venus*. I love the idea that the girl lying there being painted is looking at the painter, but he's definitely only looking at her bottom – which is fantastic. It's the reality. It was a beautiful woman that he was painting. It reflects what is in the painter's head before photography automatically taught us how to select a particular image.

Years ago I was working on *Petulia*, and I became quite

friendly with the screenwriter Larry Marcus. I remember talking to him about mirror shots, and he told me an amusing story of an incident that had once happened to him at a script meeting with a studio executive. The executive had wanted to make changes to the script and the discussion had got a bit agitated, and he said, 'Hold that thought, Larry, I just need to tell someone something,' and he got up and went round the L-shaped corner of this big office and out of sight – and Larry said he heard him mumbling behind the half-shut door. He came back a couple of minutes later and said, 'You know, I've been thinking maybe you'll do it, maybe you won't, but I think the scene needs it' – and he'd talk about the changes, then continue the meeting. Every now and then he'd say, 'Damn,' and go round the corner again, half shutting the door – then he'd come back and his behaviour was more definite or more relaxed, even letting Larry have his way. Anyway, the meeting came to an end and he said, 'I have to go, Larry – we'll pick this up in the morning,' and he walked with Larry out past the secretary to the car park. Larry said goodbye, and once he'd seen the executive walk away to his car, he went back inside up to the office and said to the secretary, 'I think I left something on the desk . . . I wonder if I could pop in and get it?' 'Oh yes,' she said, and he went back in. He just had to see what was round the corner. It was another part of the office with filing cabinets and things, but there was also a full-length mirror on the wall. Larry thought, 'Well, I'm damned – the guy must have been saying to himself: "You don't have to take this shit from Larry Marcus – you're the head of the studios."' This man had been looking into the mirror and reassuring himself that he was the boss.

The mirror in the make-up department does more for the artist than just enable them to check how their make-up is being put on. A mirror is a very magical and extraordinary thing. It was also a rather grand thing to have until the last couple of hundred years. Reflections have always been mysterious – from Narcissus looking at his reflection in a pond and becoming hypnotised by it to the story of Larry Marcus and the studio executive. But the mystery seems to be overlooked now. It's become so commonplace and such an obvious thing for everyone to live with. We are always looking at ourselves in mirrors, windows, everything, but what are we really seeing? What are we really searching for? Confidence? Various things. When people look in mirrors, they give themselves away or they're surprised – surprised at how they look.

I have always thought it would be interesting to have rehearsals where the actors were able to observe themselves in a mirror. They could watch themselves in a scene because that's what the camera does – it goes right into the face and sees whether they're lying or not – whereas on the stage actors have to exaggerate their performance.

We think of a mirror as an ordinary piece of furniture, but it's more like another eye. A mirror in the room sees things all the time. What's the phrase? 'Magic mirror on the wall' – it's usually misquoted as 'Mirror, mirror on the wall,' but it's 'Magic mirror on the wall, who is the fairest of them all?' from *Snow White*.

Mirrors are part of human existence now, certainly social existence. Wealthy women or ones up the social scale used to be dressed by servants, and the lady's maid did the hair, fastened the clothes and did the make-up. That's why they were usually overly made up – they weren't checking in a mirror. Something frosted maybe, but ordinary dwellings didn't have mirrors in them.

It's part of our existence now. Just as we weren't born with nappies and clothes, we had to learn to recognise ourselves in mirrors. That's the way we are: we were born nudists and we were born non-mirrorists.

Another thing that has struck me – vaguely linked to the magic of the mirror – is that the mirror is watching everything in the room, so it is also watching us watching each other all the time. Its magic has been very much trans-ferred now to the computer or laptop. We have been dis-tracted from 'seeing' things. I've noticed it happening in the street: people are not paying attention to things. I started to notice it long before the iPods, etc. – as far back as when we were shooting *Insignificance*, which was about a fictitious Marilyn Monroe.

We are always being watched. Someone is watching us. I like that thought. Apart from by the mirror and by someone who actually wants to know about us, we are always being watched. It's just a state of our existence. There's something about our interrelationship with society, something we don't seem to realise: we are always a part of it and alone at the same time.

A chance incident that happened to me reflected this, and

prompted me to put it into a movie. One day I was walking my dog around the block and I was on the other side of the road from a car that had pulled up. A man was sitting in it going through some papers. The ground-floor curtain of the house he'd stopped in front of had been pulled to one side, revealing a woman with an extraordinarily hard expression on her face. She was staring at the man in the car. I thought, 'What a marvellous thing, what a marvellous shot.' I was thinking in terms of movies – the expression on her face was tough and hard. I stood looking at them, pretending not to, walking the dog round in a circle but watching. Suddenly the curtain flapped back, and as I crossed the road the door of the house opened and the woman came down the steps. I was virtually ten feet from her. She banged on the window of the car, and the man looked up and smiled. He was holding some papers that he had, perhaps, brought back from the office and was working on them when she banged again. He rolled the window down, and she leant in and said, 'What were you doing in Richmond this afternoon at three o'clock?' Patently, he was stunned – suddenly the whole story came alive. He began to splutter out an answer: 'Oh, I had to get . . .' She shouted, 'Oh, shut up!' and turned round and went up the steps. He quickly gathered his things, and as he went up the stairs, she slammed the door in his face. He then opened it and went in.

It was a scene from a movie. Their movie. I thought, 'Some day I must use that scene.' Certainly he'd been spotted in Richmond – I suspect it was because of some other liaison, and maybe a friend of hers had said, 'Ooh, Charles

was in Richmond – I saw him coming out of this house.'
Who knows what it was? But it was a scene.

I put it in *The Man Who Fell to Earth*. When Mr Newton
is being interrogated, he is asked, 'Did anybody see you?'
He says, 'No.' But there was a man in a black suit, like a
CIA man, standing – just a cut of him watching – when the
rocket lands, and he sees the splash of the rocket's arrival. He
just looks and walks away. That was the 'watcher' of things,
and it's certainly so linked to movies and the camera and
CCTV – we're all being watched the whole time.

A curious coincidence – or is there no such thing as coincidence? Antony Gormley's wonderful *Angel of the North*
monument, who stands watching like many other figures he
has made, has a rather odd link to me and a movie I made
many years before: Gormley's wife is the daughter of the
couple whose farmhouse I rented for the first scene of *Don't*

The Man Who Fell to Earth: surrounded by screens

Look Now. I think it's strange that the little girl who was the daughter of that couple is now married to the sculptor Antony Gormley, whose figures watch and stare at people and places.

I don't know why I connect these odd stories to magical thought and mirrors except probably because they are, rather obviously, linked to secretly being observed like one-way glass and the camera obscura. I love that name. A while ago I was sitting on the set watching the crew set up a long tracking shot and waiting for the artists to arrive. The camera crew were checking the focus and lens and various focus settings and I thought what a wonderful thing the motion-picture camera is. What a magical machine. I came out of my pondering and said to one of the young assistants, 'Do you know why that is called a camera?' He said, 'No, what do you mean? It's just a camera . . .' 'You're right,' I said, 'it's a camera and that name goes back in time to before Aristotle, before 300 BC when its full name was the "camera obscura" – the little dark room – where images were captured and projected onto walls.' The Hockney–Falco thesis suggests that the complex but extremely accurate portrayal of some subjects from the Renaissance period in art history would hardly have been possible without the technical help of projection which could then be easily traced and painted over.

I've always felt the camera, that little dark room where images are trapped with the help of the mirror (that even more magical and ancient device) to capture images, has now also the ability to trap the movement of that reflected image and frozen time.

Oh! This could go on and on; all things and thoughts are connected.

What is next?

The future, it's already here. Time and distance. We are already playing games with it. 'Distance' is just next door . . . and 'time' is becoming one big extending moment.

The Future

I never think about the future ... it comes soon
enough.

Albert Einstein

I love film. I love the idea of it. It's still completely mystical
and mysterious to me.

I haven't had a life full of ambition. I've always been will-
ing to leap into the unknown – that way you're investing in
the future. There's compromise in everything, but you try
to hold off the compromise as long as possible. The argu-
ment against doing something is always in terms of practic-
ality. How do you argue for the unknown against something
that's established? Business people don't like dealing with
something that's completely unknown, so you get into terrible trouble. But when I look at my films now, when people
talk about my films now, I'm happy that they are still alive,
whereas some films that were tremendously successful at the
box office are moribund.

It sounds rather old-fashioned or pretentious, but in a
way the films are like one's children. Some have very sad

and difficult beginnings but they end up OK; and some might be popular but don't end up so well, but you still feel for them because they're part of your life. You can't say I prefer him because he did well, whereas she hasn't fulfilled my hopes. They're all part of 'It's my fault' – it's Dad's fault really.

I'm outside the computer/digital generation, but I can see what to use, where to shift, how to extend what's possible now. I like to think that I'm ahead of the game. If I were offered a 3D film now, I'd be excited. I'd be thinking, not 3D effects up there on a screen, but 3D in a room, with characters that stand out.

I remember going to the National Theatre to see *Pravda* – the play by David Hare and Howard Brenton about a newspaper tycoon. It was in the Olivier Theatre and Anthony Hopkins came right up to me – right up to the lip of the Olivier stage. He wasn't looking at me, he was looking beyond me, then he walked back upstage and then came down in front of me again – it was fantastic! That's what 3D should be. You'll be sitting at home, in front of a flat-screen TV and the characters will come right up to you!

I think of 3D as a much more personal movie form; it hasn't been used yet with a sense of the future. It seems to be used today as it was in the 1950s. I wouldn't be surprised if there wasn't another form of projection about to arrive. You'll turn around and see another character behind you – you'll be in the scene. The 3D movie of today will not be the 3D movie of our grandchildren's day. That movie will be completely different. Up to now we've been looking at

shadows, but now – who knows? . . . What I do know is that
you can't hang on to the past. 'The world is ever changing.
like the universe.'

I think we are entering another age of human relationships between various different 'realities' (that word has become a very confusing description). Perhaps we are not the
creatures we think we are. Between the choice of describing
ourselves as either real or artificial . . . artificial would be
thought of as the idiot's choice . . . I am an idiot.

We are fast reaching an over-designed state and for me
it all started in the simplest and most creative way. The entrapment and ability to repeat or reverse time and action in
the form of images . . . the movies. The magical power of
the movies was not really considered very much; in fact, it
was thought of as a rather lowly branch of the performing
arts. Its relationship with science, philosophy and time is not
even touched on or thought about in terms of faith and religion. But a door has been opened . . . The door to 'perhaps',
where everything must be considered possible.

Who would have believed as little as four or five hundred
years ago that we would all be able to fly? Anyone even
mentioning it as a glimpse of the future would have been
thought of as a witch or a nutcase. The only thing missing
from the idea was how we would be able to do it. The 'aero-
plane' was not even thought about as a possibility even by
scientists. Now, in less than a century, the wartime fighter pilot (that as a boy I had hoped to be) has become as outdated
as the armoured knight on horseback. The aircraft will be
– is! – controlled from a computer in an office at Air Force

HQ. There are no aerial 'dogfights'. Predicting is very difficult; it has a completely different set of 'rules of reasoning',
nearly always ridiculed. The one thing I feel a sense of truth
about is that we are entering a new era. The future is the ultimate fiction. It has no end.

Polti's *The Thirty-six Dramatic Situations* was written in
the early 1920s; around the end of an era and overlapping
the beginning of another. I have been very lucky to have
lived from the very beginning of one era; and with luck I
think I shall see the final development of it and the start
of the next ... I feel as though I am in a fictional world. I
certainly think I can imagine two or three more dramatic
situations than Polti. But then they probably wouldn't be
considered normal. But then again to quote the shrink in
Bad Timing, normal is not a word I use. I have spent a good
part of my life trying to understand what normal means and
I still don't know.

This age we are heading for began in an unrealised and
almost accidental way: the capturing of time and place with
the moving image – the movies. At first, they were only
thought of as an unsophisticated form of 'circus-like' entertainment – with the same denial of possibilities and frightening results, which are now beginning to present themselves again. But this time, like Adam and Eve, we are not
going to be able to resist temptation. How soon will it be before we are able to enter the past, and moviegoing will take
place in a dream state and in a form of personal hypnotism
... nearly everyone, at some time in their lives, has had a pre-
monition of some kind. I've always thought it's a bit like the

movies when the sound and picture get out of sync. I've had a couple of experiences like that.

Once when I was a boy of eleven or twelve, I was about to start at a new school in Brighton. I was walking on my way to the beach, the road was quite deserted, when suddenly a bus drew up beside me and I jumped on, not that I really needed to, I was only about one stop away from the sea. The bus was an open-topped double-decker and as I ran upstairs the sun came out from a cloud right in front of me and it seemed to get larger as I ran up the steps towards it. It could only have been a few seconds, even less, but in that time a whole sense of understanding came over me. Time didn't seem to exist and I felt totally relaxed and happy and I remembered everything from the past, a past I'd never had. Then almost immediately everything began to disappear from my mind. I tried to stop it, but I couldn't . . . I felt it all slide away from my thoughts . . . and I was still running on my way upstairs. In fact, I hadn't even paused and before I'd taken another step the whole memory had disappeared from my mind and everything appeared to be as it was expected to be with other people on the bus and a few cars on the road, which I had thought before had been quite empty. To this day I can only recall a feeling of 'calm' in the knowledge of the existence of a life I'd had no awareness of, either physically or emotionally.

I had a sense of wonder in suddenly understanding everything about life and death, and how obvious and simple it all was.

It was just a game that everyone was playing on their

own. Everything had been explained to me in that timeless mini-second . . . and I can't remember anything about it. As I try to describe it I am saying to myself, 'But it wasn't like that.' Maybe life is just a computer game played by an extra-terrestrial imagination. I must say, completing this era feels the same as coming to the end of a computer programme. Our controller is getting a bit bored and is about to junk it and replace it with something less obvious and stupid. Per-haps it will be given to the kids to do crazy things with be-fore they drop it in the crusher and the spirits that inhabit the characters will be released to go and inhabit other ima-gined people or creatures from a completely different time zone.

Now I am near the end of my present future and the start of another, I feel more sure (not certain) that the magical qualities of the 'movies' in their early years and their import-ant connection to the changing patterns of life and time can never be completed to an ultimate solution, in terms of our experiences. Added to this, the ability to record sound is his-torically as relevant as the alphabet is to the written word.

The technical advances and the speed at which they have come to be accepted and used by the whole spectrum of so-ciety has brought humans a serious step towards an almost 'God-like' state. There are possibly only two steps further to take. The creation of man-made machine that has:

1) an 'opinion' based on information that it has been pro-cessed to have, and
2) an opinion of its own based on information that it has

been physically 'man-given'; but coupled with emotionally guided reasoning.

That surely will be a form of 'Birth of the Future'.

That is as far as I am going. My flawed life will surely either come to an advancing heavenly state or a repeating one, depending how my needs are judged by my personal and individual God double . . . Is that science fiction?

Onwards!

Jumping away from the past . . . or into the future: the same thing?
Fahrenheit 451, 1965/6.

DISTECTA MEMBRA

DISJECTA MEMBRA

I will say of Shakespeare's works generally, that we have no full impress of him there; even as full as we have of many men. His works are so many windows, through which we see a glimpse of the world that was in him. Alas, Shakespeare had to write for the Globe Playhouse: his great soul had to crush itself, as it could, into that and no other mould. It was with him, then, as it is with us all. No man works save under conditions. The sculptor cannot set his own free Thought before us; but his Thought as he could translate it into the stone that was given, with the tools that were given. *Disjecta Membra* are all that we find of any Poet, or of any man.

HEROES AND HERO-WORSHIP
CARLYLE

We are all born ghosts of uninvited accidents and
fears; of life and sex and love and time . . .

The following is a moment of time in my life that might not
even have happened. The more distant I become from what
I think happened the more I think I might have imagined it
and it lodged, by mistake, in that part of my brain that deals
with memory.

   This is not for investigation. These are just observations
and thoughts that can easily be dismissed or ridiculed.
However – and that is a really big 'however' – there are
very many ordinary, clever, even brilliant people who wonder about similar incidents in their lives and turn them
over in their minds and often, when alone, make connections with their thoughts until they seem to make sense.
Perhaps it is linked in some way to that state the Aborigin-
als call 'Dreamtime', or as Edgar Allan Poe wrote shortly
before he died, 'Is *all* that we see or seem / But a dream
within a dream?'

   I shall call it –

Once: You Were My Mother

About ten years ago I was sitting at home on my own having a very nice martini and watching a bit of TV before sorting out some bills and going to bed.

A very ordinary evening. A nice empty-mind time. Then there was a ring and a knock at the front door ... 'Damn! Who's that? Shall I even answer it? Oh! Well! It might be important.' Standing there was an elderly women, smartly dressed, and with a rather embarrassed smiling expression on her face. She said, 'Do forgive me ... I hope I haven't disturbed you ... But are you Mr Nicholls or Nicholson?' I said, 'No ... I'm sorry you must have the wrong address.'

To which she replied, 'There is definitely no Mr Nicholls living or staying here? ... Mr Reg or Reggie Nicholls?'

At which I laughed and told her that in fact, quite curiously, my name was Nicolas Roeg.

'Ah!' she said. 'That must be it ... I've got it the wrong way round ... I would really love to talk to you for a few minutes, even if it's not tonight, I could come back another time. You don't know me, but it's about our past.'

I was a bit confused, but anyway, I invited her in. She seemed rather nice and I had a strangely good feeling about her. I had no idea who she was, but somehow I felt I knew her.

After a few more apologies and laughs at the name reversal of Reg Nicholls and Nicolas Roeg, she went on to tell me why she had come to see me and how she had found me.

Apparently, two or three weeks before, she had been in a local supermarket at the same time as me and as I brushed past her, she had had the most astonishing sense of connection, so much so that she had followed me home and the name confusion came about because she heard one of the local builders call me Mr Nicolas or Nicholls.

She then went on to explain that she was a past-life medium.

She began by telling me that past lives had no genetic connection, they were solely spiritually linked and were more connected to the third and fourth dimensions of time, which were only just beginning to be vaguely recognised in an attempt to understand eternity – although that wonderful line from *The Man Who Fell to Earth* – 'all things begin and end in eternity' – is coming closer to being the first step from a poetic thought to part of a scientific equation.

She said it is difficult to know whose past life is inhabiting us and extremely rare to make a past-life connection to a stranger, as there is absolutely no physical relationship whatsoever.

She went on to explain that after the shock of the first brush with me she went home to try and hold a private 'single' séance to find out something about my past life, knowing nothing about me. Nothing happened and for two or three weeks she gradually thought less of it and just put it down to some unknown magnetism – or maybe just an exaggerated sense of déjà vu.

She had tried to put it out of her mind, but she began to obsess about it, so she came to find me again.

As she sat down she smiled again and said, 'I'm so sorry to disturb you. I just had to have a moment of time alone in your company. I so wanted to look into your eyes on our own without anyone breaking our connection.'

She took hold of my hand and tears came to her eyes as she continued, 'Without knowing you ... I've thought of you so much over the past few years and now that we've met I feel a life has been completed and our spirits can drift on in space.'

I must say I too felt oddly at ease. I didn't want to question her or comfort her, but to sit with her, holding her hand, which felt so young and so familiar.

She explained that being able to make contact with past lives had not been something she had studied. In fact, she had never really questioned it, but understood it more as a gift – this extraordinary ability to pass through and inhabit or recognise moments of parallel time. This had gone on for many years with absolutely no involvement with personal relationships, just sensing and watching other forms of existence both historically and physically. Fascinated but detached, until one day with a great sense of shock, she realised that what she was seeing was herself in another time and body. 'In fact,' she said, 'in that past life I was watching, and being drawn to, I was a man and as that man I was thinking about my birth. I was watching my birth, or the spirit of it, and you were there or the spirit of you was there and at that moment in time you were my mother giving birth to me.'

She said, 'In calendar time it must have been about 1820, 1825. I can't exaggerate the shock of it because I quickly realised the young woman giving birth – she could only have been about nineteen or twenty – was in desperate distress. She died two or three days later. In the moments I was watching, time took on another dimension from past and present and I realised in that parallel existence two or three days had passed and I was watching from the future as that young woman died . . . . You died.'

I remember as she told me this she started to cry and it was at that moment my own sense of awareness seemed dislocated and I was conscious of being in the presence of the scene she was describing, just as though I were dreaming it. I don't know how long it lasted in real time (or rather in our time) probably only seconds, but in dreamtime I was there at that birth . . . Giving birth.

As that feeling faded and I became aware of my familiar surroundings, rather like coming round from an odd moment of dozing off, I saw that my strange caller was standing talking to me. Seemingly unaware that I'd been asleep. She was obviously getting ready to leave and finishing some conversation she'd been having with me that I'd not been conscious of. She thanked me and apologised if she had been too intrusive. She said something about meeting again, if I wanted to, but she would wait until I got in touch with her – and then she left.

I think it was only about an hour after she had left that I felt completely awake and in my present time, and I realised I had no idea who she was, what her name was or where she lived. I had no address and no phone number. I can only imagine she had given me all that information in the time my consciousness and memory were in another time and place.

I never saw or heard from her again.

It seems such a dramatic and crazy incident that I've hardly told anyone about it. I've kept it to myself as one of those secret moments of madness or coincidence that shape one's thoughts, but one hesitates to discuss – especially as it was about her and her spirit as a man in a past life from which, as the mother of that man, I was one 'life' removed.

It was only after some semi-connected conversation a little while ago about dreams and their meanings and visions of people – sometimes total strangers – that I began to talk about this incident. The Internet has transformed our dreams and imaginings into multi-secret lives, no longer only in our minds, but actually interconnecting with other people, real and imaginary – to the point of living a life in a parallel society, which becomes as real and as full as the one we have accepted and tend to believe is the real one.

Already neuroscience is proposing that we have no real identity. I believe Sebastian Faulks's novel *Engleby* concerns characters detached from reality. The thought that everyone has multiple selves, with or without the computer, must surely be based on a belief and recognition of multi-dimensional time.

I love the idea that computers have prompted our own physical computers, our brains, to link science with art and myth, old wives' tales and what we call the supernatural. I believe I read somewhere recently that by 2030 computers will have reasoning. It was not made a great deal of, I presume because it was quite an unsurprising piece of information.

When I was a boy at school (I must have been about fourteen or fifteen) we had some quite prominent people visit two or three times a term to give lectures and hold open discussions. It was during the middle of the Second World War and most of the lectures were given by admirals or generals in a thinly disguised recruitment drive for the different services. However, one of these lectures was given by a rather eminent astronomer (not for recruitment to the stars!) and I clearly remember him telling us, with great scholarly authority, how any space travel would be totally impossible as no speed or altitude could be reached or sustained outside and beyond the pull of gravity. So we could just forget about visiting the Man on the Moon . . . Oh dear! Where is he now?

I think of the programme (*Once You Were My Mother*) as a coming together of science, myth, faith, art and time – and of them being connected . . . as of course they always have been. The idea of separating science from the inventive imagination and keeping it mainly rooted in the world of proven thought denies it that wonderful quality of being constantly surprising. It is so exciting when something flies in the face of, or goes against, every truth or rule one has begun to believe in – that marvellous phrase, 'Well I'm damned! Who would have thought it?' sums it up so perfectly.

In 2008, Professor Michael Heller, a cosmologist and philosopher specialising in mathematics and metaphysics, won the Templeton Foundation Prize of £820,000 for pushing the metaphysical horizons of scientific research and discoveries about spiritual realities. His research ranges beyond Einstein into quantum mechanics, cosmology, physics and pure mathematics. Professor Kariol Musiol said of the win, 'Religion isolating itself from scientific insights is lame and science failing to acknowledge other ways of understanding the universe is blind.' Nothing can illustrate that all things and thoughts are connected more than that.

The aphorism from *The Man Who Fell to Earth* suits Professor Heller's thoughts on eternity, which argues against the Newtonian concept of creation, which is the idea that there is an absolute time and an absolute space and that energy and matter were created within a certain time-frame.

He suggests that we should look again at the whole reasoned theory of dimensions and aging and go back to the rather more ancient doctrine that the creation of the universe was an act that occurred outside space and time. It is truly a great leap to rethink our thoughts on the dimensions and realities of space and time, but then everything we believe in was unbelievable once – and the period and time is getting shorter and shorter in which things are considered unbelievable.

Basically, *Once You Were My Mother* is a sci-fi series, but sci-fi set in the present, drawing from ancient beliefs and myths stemming from thoughts and practices embracing the most other-worldly imaginings about life and death that come under the identity of reincarnation.

Is reincarnation so insane? Are the many other thoughts about death and the expectancy of what happens at the end of life any less fanciful or more provable? In fact, if anything, reincarnation of the spirit would seem more reasonable than the Paradise so many young people are committing suicide for; especially in light of the particularly mortal pleasures that are promised as reward for the super-faithful who take that tragic step.

The science-fiction writer Arthur C. Clarke once said, 'When a distinguished but elderly scientist states that something is possible, he is almost certainly right. When he states that something is impossible, he is very probably wrong.'

The retention of the moving image and the capturing of sound – with the ability to repeat and hear speeches and noises from the past and the screams of people shot and wounded on the battlefield – has been with us for only a hundred and fifty years. Now, with the coming of the age of the computer and the acceptance of being able to live parallel and second lives, one must wonder . . . is Nature giving us the first tips on what it is possible for us to understand?

I've put together these notes and thoughts about the mysteries of the present-day world because I only want to make it easier to accept the idea of past life and spiritual reincarnation and not dismiss it out of hand. Something of this kind of thought has been around since before our knowledge of the history of realities and some aspect of it has been part of almost every major religion or faith.

However, my proposed programme would not be designed to preach a theory, but only to serve as entertainment for the audience to accept or not – to question, or simply to watch, listen, and interpret as one would a dream.

In general terms, I think it could be a half-hour or forty-five minute programme during which one or two or, at the most, three people would be talked to about their lives, backgrounds and memories of childhood. Did they have any experiences of déjà vu or premonitions, etc.? It would be very interesting if we could use well-known and successful people as well as unknown, even unlucky ones.

The people selected would obviously have been examined by the past-life mediums (I think there should be two or three of those as well) and those who have been able to make connections could have their moments of contact drama-tised in a simple and semi-documentary way – similar to the example at the beginning of this treatment. It would be in-teresting to look at the time and place of the past life in a geographical and historical context to see how things have changed, or not, depending on the lapse in time of the rein-carnation. With reincarnation, there is no definitive time in terms of our accepted linear dimensions of days, months and years.

I think the dimensions of time and space should play a big part in the programme. We could not only the look at the past lives through a medium, but also at the curious cases of individuals who sense themselves, sometimes quite unwit-tingly, as having been here in the world before. I know that when one of my sons was born, my wife said, shortly after the birth, when she was feeding him and he was gazing up at her, that she had an odd feeling about his awareness. She said, 'I just know he's an old soul.' Then, one day some few weeks later, I asked her if she still felt the same way or if there were any further signs, she said, 'No ... funnily enough I watched it drift away from his eyes a few days ago.'

I'm sure the young could play a wonderful part in the programme, which would essentially be more like a computer game. It has no connection to genetics, or to race or class. Self-will is not threatened, but it does connect us to all the basic and universal dimensions of the human condition – and perhaps it hints at future ones. Even to dimensions that exist now that we just don't, won't or refuse to recognise. We are just people on our own ... But we are not alone.

Pre-existence

While sauntering through the crowded street,
Some half-remembered face I meet,

Albeit upon no mortal shore,
That face, methinks, has smiled before.

Lost in a gay and festal throng,
I tremble at some tender song –

Set to an air whose golden bars
I must have heard in other stars.

In sacred aisles I pause to share
The blessing of a priestly prayer –

When the whole scene which greets mine eyes
In some strange mode I recognize

As one whose every mystic part
I feel prefigured in my heart.

At sunset, as I calmly stand,
A stranger on an alien strand –

Familiar as my childhood's home
Seems the long stretch of wave and foam.

One sails toward me o'er the bay,
And what he comes to do and say

THE WORLD IS EVER CHANGING

I can foretell. A prescient lore
Springs from some life outlived of yore.

O swift, instinctive, startling gleams
Of deep soul-knowledge! Not as *dreams*

For aye ye vaguely dawn and die,
But oft with lightning certainty

Pierce through the dark, oblivious brain,
To make old thoughts and memories plain –

Thoughts which perchance must travel back
Across the wild, bewildering track

Of countless aeons; memories far,
High-reaching as yon pallid star,

Unknown, scarce seen, whose flickering grace
Faints on the outmost rings of space!

Paul Hamilton Hayne (1830–86)

'The centre that I cannot find
Is known to my unconscious mind;
I have no reason to despair
Because I am already there.'

W. H Auden, 'The Labyrinth'

Have we reached a point in time where we only celebrate
'modernism' and abandon all beliefs, either in established
religions or inexplicable paranormal fantasies, which appear
not to have any connection to scientific reason or provable
evidence, and which embrace the secular and atheistic culture to the point of ridiculing everything – apart from the
three prime senses.

Those two rational and useful tools – the clock and the
calendar – have for centuries dictated and set boundaries
on our ability to fantasise. Just recently an experiment at
CERN in Switzerland – which has been tested over 15,000
times – has thrown the whole of Einstein's accepted theory
of relativity into a state of confusion, even disbelief, insofar
as the nature of time is concerned – i.e. past, present and

future. It even gives credence and reason to the artistic work in film that dismays the more established creators of performance and literary media – who work strictly to the rules of storytelling – that is, one of progression in time from beginning to middle to end.

Must time always move onward? I still love the 'time zone' differences of the world. They present so many storyline situations, wonderfully put to song in Jimmy Webb's 'By the Time I Get to Phoenix'.

From the first time I sat at the Editola and ran film backwards and forwards, I've been fascinated by the idea of reversing time; in fact, every aspect of time and how we are fooled by it and all its emotional changes. I believe that film and the ability to trap the moving image and re-play it has been a big scientific step in understanding reality and existence.

Perhaps the movies hold clues to realities even bigger than Einstein or Darwin's theories.

'Science Fiction' has become a rather dated description. Film opened the door of doubt to the collapse of the difference between fiction and reality. My generation and the generation following me is still trying to believe in rules: that there is a right and wrong way of constructing and performing a story.

There is a curious duality in the mix of time and place with one person caught for a moment in the middle – then dismissing it as a freak of subconscious imagination. Quite easily understood today, but not so long ago it would have been thought to be a load of confusing storytelling.

The ability of film or television to transport your

thoughts swiftly, almost magically, from one time zone and place to another – solely with images – has become the instant pictorial remembrance. The equivalent of the written paragraph, even the page of description following, or preceding, the two written words 'he thought'.

More and more we are accepting that 'the future' is the ultimate fiction. It's impossible to predict or plan our lives. It's very rare to have our memories overlap the life and time in which we are physically living. Animals have a different attitude and sensitivity towards what we know as the progress of time. They certainly have another awareness of their surroundings and are much more able to read the moment – both visually and by sounds beyond our sight and hearing.

I love the magical ... fortune-tellers, soothsayers, prophets, déjà vu, clairvoyance. The paranormal has featured in the arts, philosophy, religion, poetry, medicine and theatre of every society and in every age from Shakespeare (*The Tempest*) to *Harry Potter*.

That old phrase, 'Nothing is for ever', seems to have a rather dated ring to it. Perhaps 'everything is for ever' and we are about to burst out of the time of 'calculated reason' into an era of revelation and the freedom of our imagination (which reason has restricted). We will be fed truths from our rebellious and secret subconscious. Our sixth sense will be positively recognised.

Colin Wilson has said that he believes one day the sixth sense will become part of the purpose of life, quite direct and un-inferred. He called it Faculty X. He thought the paradox is that we already possess it to a large degree, but are unconscious of possessing it. Or don't want to admit it, because the magical, or mystical, leap into acceptance lies at the heart of all 'occult' experience ... Why do we so fear, or try to dismiss, the unknown?

I have always felt rather lucky about the period I was born into. That is, in terms of being around in the early years of popular film-going. I started going to the local picture house with my sister when I was about eight or nine, before the Second World War. It was considered a real treat, which we spoke about afterwards for days, going over all the extraordinary things that we had seen.

Somehow, I believed that what was on the screen was real. It is difficult to express the innocent bewilderment of sitting in that big dark room watching something as exciting and 'real' as a Western, with a bunch of cowboys and Indians riding, fighting and shooting it out across the wide-open plains of America. As I sit here thinking about it, I really feel transported back in time: in memory and emotionally. Even using the very description 'cowboys and Indians' takes me back to a non-PC time ... a different era.

Recorded sound and the retention of the moving image is now so accepted that it is not considered anything more than a purely technological ability. Without any connection to the supernatural. How will it be when we are able to capture the shadows of the future?

Reason sets the boundaries far too narrowly for us and would have us accept only the known. The more 'critical reason' dominates, the more impoverished life becomes. Overvalued reason has this in common with political absolutism.

Under its dominion, the individual is pauperised and dictators are born.

Over forty years ago a man stood on the moon for the first time. The images of the Earth that were sent back from there have a strange and confusing sense of wonder about them – unlike its opposite, i.e. looking at the moon from the POV of the Earth.

At first, this might seem pretty obvious; certainly, we have come to accept it as a kind of 'general understanding' of the universe, along Darwinian/Dawkins-type lines of 'calculated' theory. However, the astronauts – in particular, Lovell and Mitchell – had unique and unusual reactions that they couldn't explain in terms of earthly comparison. Mitchell secretly experimented with extrasensory perception with two friends on Earth. He later founded the Institute of Noetic Sciences in Petaluma, California, to study what might be called the paranormal. He said it was the lunar journey that opened his eyes to something larger in the universe. He describes it as his 'ah-ha experience'. A revelation? Was it a 'Damascene' moment – Saul to Paul – that has become a bit too embarrassing to continue to explain or even talk about? Some things, if you haven't experienced them yourself, are impossible to describe accurately.

Oddly enough, when we were shooting *The Man Who Fell to Earth*, I thought it would be wonderful to have a real astronaut take part in the scene where Mr Newton – the alien played by David Bowie – is preparing to return to his own planet. Jim Lovell said he would be happy to play the part. When the time came, an extraordinary amount of people turned up to watch and ask Jim to sign photographs and dollar bills. Even hundred-dollar bills! He had such an aura about him, some people just followed him around and stared at him. Everyone seemed to be aware they were in the presence of someone who had been to places they would never go and seen things they would never see.

Even David Bowie said to me afterwards that he had felt quite strange meeting him. I'd like to include the following interview with comments from David Bowie on the experience of playing Thomas Jerome Newton. I'm obviously flattered by them, but they also have a very truthful sense about them regarding the character of the film, and perhaps, in an oblique way, the surfaces of another reality we were trying to scratch:

Believe me, I really landed on my feet with *The Man Who Fell to Earth*. I couldn't have written that sentence without Nic's brave decision to cast me as the tragic Thomas Jerome Newton. I never again worked on a movie that felt as imbued with such a sense of magic and foreboding as Nic's sci-fi classic. Even travelling back to my rented ranch house through the hauntingly beautiful desert every night after the shoot had finished was like skimming along through some kind of parallel interpretation of the film itself, so strong was Nic's creative overview. Even though I'm certain that our small crew of Englishmen seemed a bit Alice in the midst of this New Mexican cacti culture, the cowboy-heavy near-fights and insults I shamelessly avoided in the sweltering border bars helped mould me into the kind of useful alien that Nic could do something with. Fragile, fragmented and dislocated. I loved working with him.

I wanted desperately for the shoot not to finish. How much? If I'd
had my druthers, we'd still be shooting to this day!

The Man Who Fell to Earth always brings to mind Bruegel's painting and Auden's commentary on it.

About suffering they were never wrong,
The Old Masters: how well they understood
Its human position; how it takes place
While someone else is eating or opening a window or just walking
    dully along;
How, when the aged are reverently, passionately waiting
For the miraculous birth, there always must be
Children who did not specially want it to happen, skating
On a pond at the edge of the wood:
They never forgot
That even the dreadful martyrdom must run its course
Anyhow in a corner, some untidy spot
Where the dogs go on with their doggy life and the torturer's horse
Scratches its innocent behind on a tree.

In Bruegel's *Icarus*, for instance: how everything turns away
Quite leisurely from the disaster; the ploughman may
Have heard the splash, the forsaken cry,
But for him it was not an important failure; the sun shone
As it had to on the white legs disappearing into the green
Water; and the expensive delicate ship that must have seen
Something amazing, a boy falling out of the sky,
Had somewhere to get to and sailed calmly on.

W. H. Auden, 'Musée des Beaux Arts'

Landscape with the Fall of Icarus by Bruegel

As babies we hear things in the womb: music, voices and, most importantly, language. It is fascinating that unborn babies seem to understand and react to all language – perhaps all languages do have, or once had, a single tongue. Babies seem to have memory as well. Certainly, later in life – in fact, sometimes quite soon after they are born – with food, scent and touch they appear to welcome or reject many things before attempting to try them. Perhaps this indicates that, in spirit, they have known them before and the remnants of their feeling about them has carried over from another life to the area of their brain that makes decisions of this kind, but which, at this stage of their mortal existence, they can do nothing about.

There are so many strange stages of development which, until only quite recently, people either simply ignored or merely put down to empty-minded, unlearned patterns of communication. Everything a baby did, every expression, every scream, was thought to be an immediate reaction and never imagined to be rooted in the past: left over and connected to another life. On two separate occasions in my life, two different mothers of two- or three-month-old babies have said to me, in quite general conversation about their child, that they thought the baby they were nursing was (to use their expression) an 'old soul'. On one occasion, one of the mothers was quite convinced that child was a re-born spirit and had an aura of old wisdom about him. The two incidents were completely unrelated to the same belief (in the sense of spiritual reincarnation) which had been felt by the mother of one of my own sons. In an odd way, it entered my own psyche and seemed to answer many aspects of my own wonderment at the 'coming and going' of life.

But without some form of proof, how can anything be believed? We all have waves of disbelief about almost everything. Perhaps love is the most personal and saddest emotion to have doubt about: 'Do you love me?' must be one of the eternal questions form any age in any language. However, without Doubting Thomas and his need for proof, there would be no development or advance in any aspect of life – mental, physical or scientific. Doubt can inspire, as well as defeat, thought.

Robert Ripley's 'Believe It or Not' books are generally thought of as fictional comics, but they have, in fact, exploded many myths over the years and have proved to be honest, true and prescient in just as many cases. One very telling item, written around 1930, told of a French airplane that had taken off and landed without a pilot and was controlled solely by wireless. It was dismissed as some mad figment of the imagination. Perhaps it was, at the time, but everything imagined eventually does – or, at least, just might be waiting to – happen.

It's all in the timing.

Today, it is the medium of the arts and the imagination that is tipping off 'possibilities' to the sciences, rather than the other way round. Perhaps less educated and informed thought is not as hampered and restricted as that of the 'known road' . . . There is always another way.

We tend to limit ourselves, and especially our imagination, by thinking of those emotional feelings, rooted in practical materialism, as universal constants. The death of mythology gave birth to the movies, and the ability to capture the physical moment from shadows. What a wonderful and magical triumph of human imagination and reasoning. Where did the original thought of the 'possibility' come from? The root of everything has changed and been put in a different perspective. Nostalgia, speed, history and time. As Koestler puts it: 'The unthinkable phenomena of extra-sensory perception (telepathy), short-term precognition, and clairvoyance appear somewhat less preposterous in the light of the unthinkable propositions of modern physics.' Theoretical physics has become more and more occult, leaning toward supernatural concepts such as negative mass, holes in space, and time flowing backwards – the flashback in films becomes a truth.

The programme should not only be centred around and

illustrated by dramatic re-enactments or 'of the moment' scenes of supernatural or occult investigation, but included with, or alongside, fictional scenes which appear convincing enough to be true, but are either constructed by cinematic special effects or performed by a great illusionist like Derren Brown. We might even manage to convince, or prompt, doubt in a sceptic. After all, the greatest sci-fi writers turn out to have been Einstein, Planck, Schrodinger and Heisenberg – coupled with philosophers such as Schopenhauer, Kammerer and Jung.

Perhaps Dawkins, and his belief in our own physical evolution, has a scientific truth, but I don't really mind whether or not, over the past few hundred million years, I am the descendant of a sardine or a monkey. When I ponder eternity, the thing that truly interests me is the future – where am I going in the next few million seconds, minutes, hours, days, months and years ... whatever they mean? And whichever order or direction they take when defining our existence.

At last the secret is out, as it always must come in the end,
The delicious story is ripe to tell to the intimate friend;
Over the tea-cups and in the square the tongue has its desire;
Still waters run deep, my dear, there's never smoke without fire.

Behind the corpse in the reservoir, behind the ghost on the links,
Behind the lady who dances and the man who madly drinks,
Under the look of fatigue, the attack of migraine and the sigh
There is always another story, there is more than meets the eye.

For the clear voice suddenly singing, high up in the convent wall,
The scent of the elder bushes, the sporting prints in the hall,
The croquet matches in summer, the handshake, the cough, the
    kiss,
There is always a wicked secret, a private reason for this.

W. H. Auden, 'At Last the Secret Is Out'

There's none so blind as they that won't see

There's no such thing as coincidence. If I hadn't bumped into the crew in the bar I would never have shot the movie in the way that I did . . .

Byron, Milton, Titian, Casanova, Napoleon etc., the list of lovers of Venice is endless, but then so is the list of those who exile themselves and pledge never to return. Venice is a mystery, it is almost essential to be introduced to it by a living and loving Venetian who can show you, with the right attitude, one of the most original and beautiful cities set in a man-made landscape – one never naturally intended to be inhabited by humans or exploited in the way it is.

In the novella *Don't Look Now* John and Laura go on holiday to Venice as a stage of recovering from the death – from an illness, not drowning – of their daughter. Naturally, the holiday was also a good way of showing and staging the scenes in identifiable tourist locations . . . St Mark's Square, Santa Maria della Salute, the Rialto Bridge and the Doge's Palazzo. It all seemed very simple and rather obvious. Then, when I arrived in Venice, two strange things happened. I met a man in a bar who, having once been a guide, told me that some of the locations we were thinking about using for the film would be very expensive to shoot in now, as Venice was becoming a very sought-after location; also we would have to get permission from the Church authorities, who would have to approve the script! Not a happy thing for me to have to do. Anyway, one of those 'life and thought' moments came upon me when I got back to the hotel that evening. There in the lobby was a bunch of film people, English and Italian, who had just got back from a location recce for a movie they were about to start in three or four weeks' time – and we hadn't even finalised the raising of the money for the basic budget of our film. I vaguely knew a couple of them, who enthused to me about how much they had found that was so visually beautiful; they joked about how far advanced they were and that I would have to find angles and views after they had finished with them ... Which would be difficult because they would have shot the shit out of them!

This may seem irrelevant, but the next morning we were going to look at the Doge's Pallazo to see if I thought something about it might be useful. We had also got permission to shoot in areas that had hardly ever been used – including where Casanova had been imprisoned, which would have been great for another movie ... but, when we arrived, an incident happened that opened a door in my thoughts. As we went into the Great Hall of the Palazzo there was a group of tourists ahead of us who were being given the 'official tour'. We had a special guide of our own. When the tourists left, our man began to tell us of the general uses of the Great Hall and the famous trials that had been held there – Casanova's, of course, being one of them. About half way through his talk, my 'tourist' eyes and ears had begun to wander and I was looking at the portraits of all the previous Doges that lined the walls at ceiling height. One of the paintings that intrigued me was covered by a rough hessian cloth, so I said to our guide, 'Why is that portrait covered? Is it being cleaned or repaired?' To which the guide replied, '*Repaired!* Certainly not! That man betrayed Venice, he is not to be looked at ... You want to see him?' I said, 'Well, I wouldn't mind.' He said, 'Wait a moment 'til the other party has completely left and we are on our own.'

When they had gone he went to another part of the hall and picked up a long pole lying on the floor against the wall; it had a big hook on the end. As he came back, I realised I was just another nosey tourist who had fallen into a very simple 'Guide Game'. The location man I was with whispered, 'I think you ought to give him something ... ' and he suggested a reasonable sum. Then the museum guide raised the pole with the hook and pushed up the covering cloth to expose the head and shoulders of a bearded man, almost identical in features and clothing to all of the others surrounding the top of the Great Hall. The location tour was over.

Almost at the same time as we were leaving, our associate producer/location manager told me of a church he had found on which he felt sure he would be able to make a reasonable deal and he really hoped I would like it.

I couldn't believe it when we got there. The church was situated on the Isle of Dorsoduro, right on the far western tip and was, at the time, in a rather run-down area and in the process of being restored. The church was named after St

Nicolo dei Mendicoli (St Nicolas of the Poor and Beggars!)
What could be more inviting than that?

The bones of the saint were in a casket at the foot of the
altar and the complete restoration of the church was being

funded by the English 'Venice in Peril' fund – which could almost be a subtitle for *Don't Look Now*. Fate and Chance had begun to take over the movie. One other seeming 'co-incidence' was that on the wall of the church, close to the entrance, there was a film poster advertising an old Charlie Chaplin film that was showing at a local cinema. I couldn't resist filming it. In fact, we track past it as John (Donald Sutherland) and the Bishop (Massimo Serato) walk away from the church. The Italian title on the poster was *Uno Contro Tutti*. How true that turned out to be.

Venice became my friend . . . I gave myself to it and Venice opened the door to secrets more personal and sensual than the familiar grand, 'man-made' surface beauty that acts as its protective shell. It is difficult to explain the reason why, but I think of Venice a lot in a fond and intimate way.

In my beginning is my end

[...]

Home is where one starts from. As we grow older
The world becomes stranger, the pattern more complicated
Of dead and living. Not the intense moment
Isolated, with no before and after,
But a lifetime burning in every moment
And not the lifetime of one man only
But of old stones that cannot be deciphered.
There is a time for the evening under starlight,
A time for the evening under lamplight
(The evening with the photograph album).
Love is most nearly itself
When here and now cease to matter.
Old men ought to be explorers
Here and there does not matter
We must be still and still moving
Into another intensity
For a further union, a deeper communion
Through the dark cold and the empty desolation,

The wave cry, the wind cry, the vast waters
Of the petrel and the porpoise. In my end is my beginning.

T. S. Eliot, 'East Coker'

'Where shall I begin, please your Majesty?' he asked.

'Begin at the beginning,' the King said, very gravely, 'and go on till you come to the end: then stop.'

Lewis Carroll,
Alice's Adventures in Wonderland

Portrait of Nicolas Roeg and Theresa Russell (Snowdon/Camera Press)

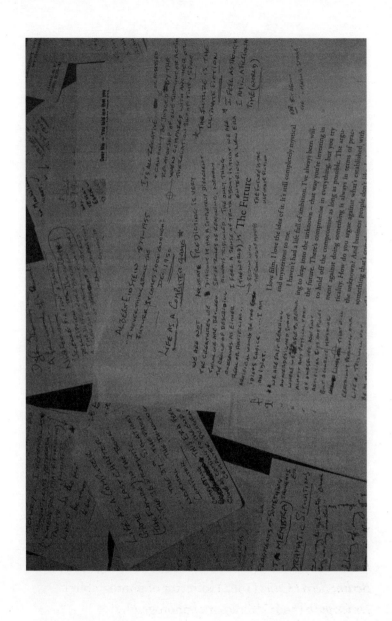

Filmography

Credited Titles

Calling Bulldog Drummond (1950) [assistant camera]
Cosh Boy (1952) [focus puller]
John Wesley (1953) [assistant camera]
Bhowani Junction (1956) [assistant camera]
Pacific Destiny (1956) [focus puller]
Passport to Shame (1958) [camera operator]
The Child and the Killer (1959) [camera operator]
Tarzan's Greatest Adventure (1959) [camera operator]
The Great Van Robbery (1959) [camera operator]
Jazz Boat (1959) [camera operator]
Doctor Blood's Coffin (1960) [camera operator]
The Trials of Oscar Wilde (1960) [camera operator]
Information Received (1961) [director of photography]
Band of Thieves (1962) [director of photography]
Lawrence of Arabia (1962) [second unit photography]
Berlin: Secret Cities (1962) [director of photography]
Dr Crippen (1962) [director of photography]
A Prize of Arms (1962) [writer: original story]

The Caretaker (1963) [director of photography]

The System (1963) [director of photography]

  Death Drums Along the River (1963) [writer: screenplay]

Just for Fun! (1963) [photography]

Every Day's a Holiday (1964) [director of photography]

Nothing But the Best (1964) [director of photography]

Judith (1964) [second unit director; additional photography]

Victim Five (1964) [director of photography]

The Masque of the Red Death (1964) [photography]

Doctor Zhivago (1965) [director of photography: some scenes]

Fahrenheit 451 (1966) [director of photography]

A Funny Thing Happened on the Way to the Forum (1966) [director of photography]

Calling Bulldog Drummond, 1950

Breakthrough (1966) [photography]

Far from the Madding Crowd (1967) [director of photography]

Casino Royale (1967) [additional photography]

Petulia (1968) [director of photography]

Schweppes Vodka Mint Cocktail 'Fiara' (1969) [director]

Performance (1970) [director; director of photography]

Walkabout (1970) [director; photography]

Nightmare Honeymoon (1972) [director]

Don't Look Now (1973) [director]

Glastonbury Fayre (1973) [director; director of photography]

Guinness – Hop Farm (1974) [director]

The Man Who Fell to Earth (1976) [director]

Bad Timing (1980) [director]

Puffball, 2007

Dallas through the Looking Glass (1981) [director]

Eureka (1982) [director]

Atmospherics (1983) [director]

Nicolas Roeg: A Guardian Lecture (1983) [on-screen participant]

Nicolas Roeg: A Guardian Interview (1983) [interviewee]

Nothing Is As It Seems: The Films of Nicolas Roeg: Visions (1983) [on-screen participant]

The Pros and Cons of Hitchhiking (1984) [live action director]

The Making of Nicolas Roeg's 'Insignificance' (1984) [interviewee]

Insignificance (1985) [director]

Castaway (1986) [director]

Getting that Break (1986) [cast member]

Aria (1987) [director: segment 'Un ballo in maschera'; writer: segment 'Un ballo in maschera']

Track 29 (1987) [director]

The Witches (1989) [director]

Sweet Bird of Youth (1989) [director]

Without You I'm Nothing (1990) [executive producer]

Cold Heaven (1992) [director]

Heart of Darkness (1993) [director]

Paris, October 1916: The Young Indiana Jones Chronicles (1993) [director]

Strangers in the City: Hollywood UK British Cinema in the Sixties (1993) [interviewee]

The Last Wave: Hollywood UK British Cinema in the Sixties (1993) [interviewee]

Two Deaths (1994) [director]

Close Up (1995) [on-screen participant]

Full Body Massage (1995) [director]

Francois Truffaut: The Man Who Loved Cinema (1996) [on-screen participant]

Samson and Delilah (1996) [director]

Sound: Sound on Film (2000) [director; writer]

Beginnings: Watching (2000) [on-screen participant]

Julie Christie: Legends (2001) [on-screen participant]

Puffball (2007) [director]

The Fan Club (unrealised) [director]

Chicago Loop (unrealised) [director]

Master of Lies (unrealised) [director]

The Guardian Interview: Nic Roeg (undated) [interviewee]

Hotel Paradise: Erotic Tales (1995) [director]

A Prize of Arms (1961) [story by Nicolas Roeg and Kevin Kavanagh]

Music Credits

Bad Timing: 'Time Out' (1980) [lyrics]

Puffball: 'Red Haired Woman' (2006) [lyrics]

Credits

Images

Photographs from *Don't Look Now* and *The Man Who Fell to Earth* courtesy of Studio Canal.

The copyright for the photographs courtesy of the Kobal Collection are held by: SGF/Gaumont (*Napoleon*); Warner Bros (*The Treasure of Sierra Madre*, *The Witches*); Max Raab/Si Litvanoff Films (*Walkabout*); Grand Pictures/Dan Films (*Puffball*); ITV Global (*Insignificance*, *Bad Timing*); Columbia (*Lawrence of Arabia*, *The Lady from Shanghai*); Anglo Enterprise/Vineyard (*Fahrenheit 451*), Caretaker Film (*The Caretaker*).

Portrait of Nicolas Roeg and Theresa Russell (Snowdon/ Camera Press).

All other photographs courtesy of the author's collection.

The Boulevard de Clichy under Snow (oil on canvas), 1876, by Norbert Goeneutte (1854–94), Tate Images, London

The Rokeby Venus, *c*.1648–51 (oil on canvas) by Diego

Rodriguez de Silva y Velázquez (1599–1660), National Gallery, London, UK/The Bridgeman Art Library

Landscape with the Fall of Icarus, c.1555 (oil on canvas), Pieter Bruegel the Elder (*c.*1525–69), Musees Royaux des Beaux-Arts de Belgique, Brussels, Belgium / Giraudon / The Bridgeman Art Library

Text

'Summer Movies' © Jeffrey Eugenides. The article first appeared in the *New Yorker*

Letter to Nicolas Roeg © Paul Theroux

'A Child in the Eighties' © Derwent May

'The Spell of the Yukon' © The Estate of Robert W. Service (William Krasilovsky, attorney)

'The Labyrinth'; 'At Last The Secret is Out'; 'Musée des Beaux Arts' © 1941; 1936; 1940 by W. H. Auden, renewed. Reprinted by permission of Curtis Brown Ltd

Extract from 'East Coker' taken from *Four Quartets* © Estate of T. S. Eliot, and reprinted by permission of Faber & Faber Ltd

Thanks are due to Harriett Harper and Samantha Matthews for their vital contributions to this book.

BRITISH ACADEMY
OF FILM AND TELEVISION ARTS

Nic Roeg: A BAFTA Tribute

On 27 March 2009, BAFTA hosted a tribute to Nicolas Roeg at its 195 Piccadilly headquarters.

Filmmakers including Danny Boyle, Peter Jackson, Christopher Nolan, Paul Greengrass, Terry Gilliam and Guillermo Del Toro paid tribute to the cinematic visionary, offering personal insights into why they've found Roeg's work inspirational.

Listen/Watch

You can download Nic Roeg's BAFTA Tribute as a podcast for free from iTunes or watch video highlights from the event, including Danny Boyle and Christopher Nolan's tributes, on www.bafta.org/heritage/features.

About BAFTA

BAFTA's vision is to support, develop and promote the art forms of the moving image, by identifying and rewarding excellence, inspiring practitioners and benefiting the public.

As a charitable organisation, giving our members, the industry and the public the opportunity to learn first-hand from leading practitioners in the film, television and games industries, via our year-round learning and events programme, is one of our key activities.

CREDITS

Amongst our other activities are our annual Awards ceremonies, held in the UK, which set the gold standard for industry practitioners everywhere.

Find out more about BAFTA on www.bafta.org or visit BAFTA Guru to watch some of the best in the industry, including Martin Scorsese, Meryl Streep, Kenneth Branagh and Charlie Kaufman, talk about their work: www.bafta.org/guru.

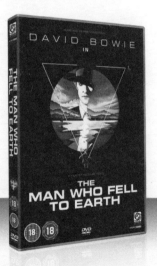